Novel

Wicked Soul

Do

"Revenge and Break"

Righteous Soul
Living Actor

SEONG JU CHOI

AuthorHouse™
1663 Liberty Drive
Bloomington, IN 47403
www.authorhouse.com
Phone: 1 (800) 839-8640

Because of the dynamic nature of the Internet, any web addresses or links contained in this book may have changed since publication and may no longer be valid. The views expressed in this work are solely those of the author and do not necessarily reflect the views of the publisher, and the publisher hereby disclaims any responsibility for them.

Any people depicted in stock imagery provided by Getty Images are models,
and such images are being used for illustrative purposes only.
Certain stock imagery © Getty Images.

This book is printed on acid-free paper.

ISBN: 978-1-7283-2969-7 (sc)
ISBN: 978-1-7283-2970-3 (e)

Print information available on the last page.

Published by AuthorHouse 09/30/2019

authorHOUSE®

Why I write wicked soul story

I know wicked soul's "revenge and break" so that I'm so fear of wicked soul near me, this is mind level living actor explain only, but actually, in the righteous soul living actor. Living in the same place, righteous soul and wicked soul is living in "ME".

I'm living for the purpose loving wicked soul to make righteous soul so the in me only living "righteous soul".

Why I try to do "novel wicked soul do "revenge and break righteous soul living actor" is my righteous soul living actor keep awakening not to be attacked from wicked soul.

Even I'm a righteous soul; this means all of macro concept world living actors are same. But truly I will do experiment "me" as the actor is "wicked soul" and "righteous soul" moving in "ME".

Here is "righteous soul" living is doing real love wicked soul, but wicked soul living is "revenge and break".

Because righteous soul created from righteous soul living in destination place bring lover to the righteous soul living in destination place, but wicked soul is wait to revenge that makes wicked soul in the cause of living.

So that wicked soul cause of being wicked soul sources all to be revenge and break, this fear of power living actor wicked soul also living in "me".

I will see in me "wicked soul and righteous soul living" in the point of righteous soul living.

I have to live righteous soul living but also my all of living grow righteous soul living energy and matured living, to do real love wicked soul even dangerous of wicked soul's revenge and break.

Why write book is without writing my living lived by wicked soul living so that, at least my writing time is feel righteous soul living.

Because righteous soul living actor meets strong righteous soul to write this book, truly even my writing in my hand but all of writing is strong righteous soul helping "ME" and sometimes my righteous soul living actor hear "broadcasting from righteous soul living in destination place.

So long, writing this book is just like strength righteous soul energy, same as physical strength body building, bodybuilding is writing.

At last this book start voyage, this book must be completed by strong righteous soul helping me every writing micro concept point. Micro concept point is micro concept tunnel to bring creature knowledge bring from righteous soul living in destination place.

(Before writing this book)

This is after writing this book, wicked soul try to help me, then I helped from wicked soul, then all is suffer from all around of me, nearby a man keep make hard, even he do not like me, but start this book so make hard.

He is superior to me, he is good at law, so then his talking all related with law, but also, his wicked soul is being strong, righteous soul "ME" so hard with him, so that I will move a new position.

If I live with him, then I feel living in hell. So that I try to keep much more writing on the position of wicked soul, but I'm feeling die.

I'm living in righteous soul, so as living righteous soul wicked soul living behavior is so hard to living.

last year final day I was so hard feeling me, truly micro concept world all occupied by wicked soul, so to survive my righteous soul, this book abruptly finish.

Because I want to live in righteous soul in safe, so then on today I will make end.

Righteous soul "ME" feeling wicked soul is itself is hell, so fear and hard to live.

Heavenly father please save me from wicked soul.

(After written this book)

Contents

Voyage 1day

Macro concept world me must be as righteous soul with wicked soul, how hard macro concept "ME". This means that righteous soul me must do real love wicked soul me. Wicked soul "me" is so sensitive to righteous soul "ME" if righteous soul says "I love you" the wicked soul "me" fully discriminate real love or false love.

So that righteous soul do real love to the wicked soul "me" then wicked soul getting slowly changed into righteous soul, but if righteous soul sleeping time, wicked soul being anger and revenger and break then wicked soul energy abruptly strong power, then wicked soul keep strong wicked soul.

Righteous soul role play is to do real love wicked soul, so that righteous soul living actor keeps diligence and awakening.

if do well, wicked soul be loved from righteous soul, so then wicked soul gradually getting better to be righteous soul living.

I want to say, my macro concept world living actor do real love wicked soul then wicked soul to be being righteous soul living. in this living truly "all from me no other" but also to be live righteous soul living it must be "there is no mind, there is no me", so long here is mind is greedy mind so then, macro concept me is mind is1/, almost to zero then, even seen body from other but the body is shelter so that truly there is no me.

In macro concept world natural living actor is governed from mind=, so called natural living actor in the macro concept world, they do not know "wicked soul, or righteous soul". So that in this novel called them as natural living actor.

Natural living actor and wicked soul living actor, but also righteous soul living actor is mixed living in the macro concept world.

Here is macro concept world is seen world, micro concept world is unseen world is easy understanding.

Just today is start voyage of this book, so that keep me awaken righteous soul living actor.

Micro concept me is going excitement. This is so good, because I did stop writing, in the micro concept world wicked soul did revenge and break so that macro concept "ME" abruptly got a sick of "facial paralysis" for 5 month I did not writing, but today after 5 months I'm starting writing, so then righteous soul living actor must be so excitement.

Voyage 2days

"Righteous soul" this word is always "ME", I have been suffered from around of me, wicked souls. Probably nature actors are all exciting of wicked soul living, this is "easy living". Righteous soul living is "it shared time with others help other and doing real love other". Living righteous soul living is keep awaken to do real love wicked soul, but natural living actor, do not know existence of righteous soul and wicked soul, so that they living in ignorance.

Last night I heard from work place colleague "meet out of wife friend", he said that out of wife a woman meeting is so good. This is living in the natural living actor. Truly righteous soul living world is difference from mind level living actor living. Their living is doing now know truth of righteous soul living creation of knowledge.

Natural people ignorance means that time used for easy living, sometimes drinking "soju" and meet woman who is meet at night.

Ignorance natural living actors are saying " to do solving stress", righteous soul living of "it shared time with other and help other but also real love other" is doing hard, sacrifice living. How to righteous soul living actor being rest and doing excitement, it is really care me, my living is broken ignorance living of easy living excitement.

This is "silly" if I pure righteous soul then I must be living in excitement with righteous soul, doing righteous soul is "spring of new and creature of water", Righteous soul living itself is excitement living, but truly I am not a righteous soul living, so it required me to live righteous soul living.

At last my source of excitement is beginning, righteous soul living actor excitement is doing role of "spring of clean new water creating" so that my writing is the same as "spring of water". This is itself is excitement living.

Role player of righteous soul is living in righteous soul, so long truly righteous soul living actor only living in the macro concept world, then micro concept world, or righteous soul living in destination place, righteous soul see only me, because righteous soul living actors are all meet in the "micro concept point or tunnel".

If natural me is living easy living, then the living is not recognition to the righteous souls in the micro concept world. Living itself is it is, if an actor live natural living then his living is limited righteous soul living actors creation of knowledge, without this righteous soul living knowledge then, it must be living is "strong mind" who is truly not organism but mind is control natural living actor, "getting much more than others", this is natural living actor living truth.

Macro concept world living actor of mind level living actor all follows "strong mind of god" this is not existed anyplace, but this is truth to the mind level living actors.

This is so dangerous living, because of their living is only living of "macro concept world" so that mind level living actor all of effort is not related with micro concept world so that their living all is doing nothing.

Because mind level living actors strong getting power is strong follow of "strong mind of god" in this place there is no "god" in this place god is not, because god is in the righteous soul, "it shared time with others and doing help other, but also doing real love others" this is same of micro concept world of righteous soul living in the righteous soul living in destination place.

Righteous soul living actor all living of macro concept world and micro concept world so that, righteous soul living actor knew that micro concept world living, so that in the macro concept world living world, righteous soul living do carry of micro concept world righteous soul living in destination place "mission what is make lover righteous soul and safe bring back to the righteous soul living in destination place with lover to live eternity in the righteous soul living in destination place.

Righteous soul living in the macro concept world to carry mission so hard, there is no time used out of it, righteous soul living is progress, "the poor & righteous soul" "righteous soul & nothing" here is macro concept world terms are "the poor" and "nothing" but micro concept world terms is "righteous soul", so long, righteous soul living actor in the macro concept world, to grow righteous soul living energy to do real love "wicked soul" so that it required of living the poor and righteous soul living, while wicked soul living actor of "easy living is top purpose" so that wicked soul living actor use power of "revenge and break".

So that righteous soul living actor must be distance from wicked soul, so long, the poor & righteous soul living is micro concept world mission carry.

Micro concept place mission is " survive in a soul room, righteous soul living actor keep doing real love so survive as righteous soul, so I'm righteous soul this is in me, but as strong righteous soul living actor meet and find "lover" who is not known whether lover is righteous soul or wicked soul living.

If righteous soul living then both righteous soul living actor already knew micro concept world mission, then they live in macro concept world do live same as micro concept world, of righteous soul living "it shared time with others, help others but also doing real love others" so long both righteous soul living actor living macro concept world living excitement.

But lover is not righteous soul living then, righteous soul living actor meet wicked soul living, then righteous soul living actor to do carry micro concept world mission, so that righteous soul living actor all do real lover the wicked soul of lover.

This is righteous soul living macro concept world and micro concept world, how time is not out of righteous soul living, so that all of effort living macro concept and micro concept world living.

If natural living actor "my living is on my way who teach me this is nothing to me" this is ignorance living, then the living is not carry micro concept mission "find lover make lover righteous soul, and safe returning to the righteous soul living in destination place.

Macro concept world living is natural living is only to be rich is purpose, but righteous soul living is infer of possible "the poor & righteous soul living".

The poor & righteous soul living is "it shared time with other, help other but also doing real love others".

Every day living is not simple, but it required living macro concept world and micro concept world all both living is required.

Voyage 3days

Today morning I did SNS with my wife, so that "ME" righteous soul try to help wife small energy of righteous soul, on today I sent to my wife "my living in excitement depends and living in excitement also depends"

This is in the saying of macro concept world wicked soul and natural living actors making sarcastic remark "love, what is making money".

At now in the macro concept world "love is meaning word just love is in the pure love comic and novel word, there is no real living world.

Love word is already old and dead word of real living. So long in the youth using love is changed words are living so long love is contaminated so that in the natural living actors "love" is not give inspired excitement. "my living in excitement depending your real loving me, and your living in excitement is depending my real loving me"

Mind is about to zero, then almost being appeared up "righteous soul "ME", this is all of macro concept world living actor same, because wide and strong influence to the body, as mind is about to zero then the big space is occupied by righteous soul, at last righteous soul feeling is micro concept world why start voyage to the macro concept world.

Being soon righteous soul living actor realized micro concept world living mission "bring lover to the righteous soul living in destination place"

So then, Righteous soul living behavior is "it shared time with other and help other and doing real love other", all of excitement is by product from living in righteous soul living behavior.

Truly righteous soul "ME" is it based on micro concept world, so that micro concept world is center of living actor is truly, unseen world of micro concept world.

So long it must be infer that natural living actors all governed from mind is only living in macro concept world of seen world.

Mind is only in the macro concept world of body, but mind is not existence in the micro concept world, but righteous soul is living with body of macro concept world of unseen world living role player, but righteous soul in the micro concept world, just living seen among righteous soul living in the righteous soul living in destination place.

Until do not mind is not zero then, natural living actor express good mind, and bad mind, this is mind only mind is even best mind but it is mind, so long mind is macro concept world living with body, so that mind is not related with micro concept world, mind is greedy so that mind make natural living actor be salver living. all of time for use making money, that is feeling safe, if living whole of time follow of mind then the natural living actor wicked soul, or righteous soul being dead in the micro concept world. I do not know but infer that mind level dead means that wicked soul living in destination place automatically belong in to wicked soul living in the end.

So long, righteous soul living actor living is save natural living actor to be living in righteous soul living in destination place.

Truly righteous soul living in micro concept world, save love from wicked soul living being, lover is truly in the natural living actor is love of family, it is same, but some difference feeling is love is macro concept world and micro concept world all living principle of doing real love so that some what difference from natural living actors in the macro concept world.

Righteous soul "ME" is all the time living with macro concept world, natural living of family, work place, so long, feeling of righteous soul living is all of communication and behavior then,

Righteous soul "ME" living is giving excitement as doing righteous soul living behavior " it shared time with other, help other, and doing real love other".

But truly, if righteous soul living "ME" is sleeping, do not awaken then around living natural, wicked soul living actors are attacking me, this is so hard to live on, "righteous soul "ME" so hard to live with them. If "righteous soul "ME" sleeping then it must be I were so dangerous from natural living or wicked souls. Especially wicked soul living actor to be "easy living" it must be clearly used wicked soul energy of "revenge and break" me, so that I must be hard living.

In the macro concept world, natural living actor, wicked soul living actor, and righteous soul living actor, but all of living actor recognized as "righteous soul "ME" then, to live from others, how to live is only living is "it shared time with other, and help other but also doing real love other", it is only to survive righteous soul living, if righteous soul living sleeping then righteous soul living energy decreased so that righteous soul living energy to make increasing, it must living awaken.

In the micro concept world, righteous soul living is truly to survive from wicked soul, always to live righteous soul living behavior "it shared time with other, help other, but also doing real love other".

In the macro concept world natural living actor all "give and take" living of based on mind level living actor behavior " it getting much more than others", so that trade is all of living criterial living.

If this is making money rule adopt but sadness culture, art, all of living is trade is standard.

In the micro concept world righteous soul living is just giving there is no accept, all is giving is all, so that it must be "righteous soul "ME" must be from other righteous soul behavior so that I'm living in the end living of righteous soul living is just "giving", donation, each other giving is righteous soul living in destination place, so excitement living.

This is same feeling of natural living actor be party from invited from party host, the as guest living is so excitement, because in the trade of mind natural living actor, just without giving my money but I eat delicious food, so that the excitement is high, but this is not usual, but also, long built good relationship then it comes party guest.

But micro concept world righteous soul living behavior "it shared time with other, help other, but also doing real love other" then living itself is so excitement living.

In real living I'm giving truly without give and take, but I'm just giving so that giving excitement is so huge, in the purchase time also I'm giving my money, so that as possible as I can select the poor of seller in the market, my purchase is giving my money so that it must not discount but also to get many getting.

Some other behavior doing but hidden my righteous soul living behavior is doing practice in my real living. This is secret, if after this book sell then a reading actor ask then I will do reply kindly.

Voyage 4days

Why field flowers are blossomed? This problem answer righteous soul living world. Then righteous soul living behavior "it shared time with flower and helping flower, but also doing real love flower"

On today morning on my way work place, walking road then then by the road hill wild flowers are all smiles for me. It is really excitement to me, my righteous soul feel really excitement, then "thank you flowers, I love all of flowers" keep repeating walked to my work place.

On my way work place, my righteous soul feels excitement, and heard broadcasting from righteous soul living in destination place.

Living righteous soul looked forward to seeing macro concept world flowers seeing excitement before living getting body in the micro concept world.

Why filed flowers are blossomed? Flower blossom role player is giving "beauty excitement" this really excitement source huge around of me every day seasonal flowers, today I feel so excitement.

Again way do not feel excitement before? It must be infer that if I were natural actor, or wicked soul living actor, or still growing to righteous soul of my righteous soul living energy was not enough.

Here is strange thing creation of knowledge occur to righteous soul "ME", it must be living in already righteous soul living in destination place, may be? All around are creature of excitement living condition is already prepared.

The problem is? my living is natural living of "getting much more than others" or wicked soul living of "easy living using revenge power and break other" but also I'm hurry to be enough, strong righteous soul living energy, "the poor & righteous soul living" is not reach at "righteous soul & nothing", but truly living condition is all equipped for righteous soul living in destination place.

Whether "me" is righteous soul, wicked soul, natural living actor, all is mixed, but it must be why field flowers are open blossomed to me then I must be "righteous soul & god" to the flowers, in the broadcasting saying "righteous soul" must be god to the flowers, further more plants because all of plants do exclusively for righteous soul "ME".

Then righteous soul "ME" do giving living "it shared time with flowers and doing helping well growing all of flowers, but also doing real love them"

To live excitement with flowers then righteous soul "ME" must do gardening, pruning and apply fertilizer of helping flowers well growing.

Here is wild flower blossom is must be righteous soul living actor od of them, so that just going with excitement, just simple watching wild flowers then saying " saying I love you, and thank" then wild flower role and replied to the good express is role to the flowers, this is role of righteous soul "ME"

Righteous soul "me" is appeared up point of seeing flowers.

Today righteous soul "Me" learning that seeing flower is also exclusively flower role to give excitement, so that flower role and righteous soul "me" role must be doing.

Flower role is good growing and beautiful flower being blossom and righteous soul "me" role play is living in righteous soul "it shared time with other, and help other, but also doing real love other'.

If flower role playing is good but there is no righteous soul around the flower then flower feeling then "heavenly father I'm beauty blossoming but there is no watch me please help me to see me righteous soul living actor see and excitement"

Flower role is keep doing well, but righteous soul living actor do not well role playing, then flower is do hard.

So long, righteous soul living actor "ME" seeing flower then saying "you are so beautiful, I'm really thank you and I love you" this saying repeated, this is righteous soul "ME" done of role playing.

Voyage 5days

Why Righteous soul me excitement ratio is changing? Every day living is not same. It must be up & down of cycle is keep change.

Righteous soul "ME" living with others who are now wicked soul, natural living actor or righteous soul living actor, here is must be if I meet wicked soul then my righteous soul energy will be decreased, but if I be meeting natural living actor then average living, but righteous soul living then righteous soul living will be increasing.

So that every day my living is how to save my righteous soul living or not is depend on every excitement ratio is vary. Today morning I'm still not excitement, on right before I said to my work place "good morning" then I was so what I feel reluctant to do but I did, then his reply to me " I have to follow your order, it means that why I have to say "good morning".

This is somewhat difference here is not English using region, but that is I feel that is he did not accept me my saying, he refuse me my trials, my intention is to make peace, but he do not accept me my proposal "good morning".

This is strongly shot of me, so then this is out of body source of decreased righteous soul living energy. in this living place all is not righteous soul, but there is wicked soul living actor also, most living is natural living actors. So long every day I try to make mind to be zero, so that "mind one per limitless of routine saying" to be peace in me.

Around of me east, west, south, north are around of me, just one is living righteous soul living then, it must be my living is living better.

My work place is not ideal living, all is really to live their hard living exodos, they are not consider others. So that this is some of living actor saying "living is survive game", this is competition is doing real so that macro concept world is accepted living of wicked soul living is normal living.

Endless competition is understand by natural living actors, so that to get much more than other is criteria, so that no one feeling of guilty.

There is no philosophical principle but only living in mind level living of "getting much more than others", my living place disappeared manners of greeting.

in my living around of just closed place, no one do manners of greeting, so that whoever all of living is "mind level of mind is full" so long, just they all follow wining position any place, the principle is "getting much more than others".

Righteous soul living is "it shared time with other, and help others but also doing real love others" as long as I'm living in righteous soul living. endless completion of there is no manners of greeting, all of living greeting is dead of real manners of greeting, then who will not give me excitement living, so then my living of righteous soul living is so hard.

I can hear of macro concept world some people died, then himself try to do disappeared from this endless competition, there is no charity so that fallen to the endless living of loser from endless competition actor must be dead.

This living is truly right or if this is not right, then it must be this living all false living lead by the mind, mind is nothing, but all of macro concept world living actors do as mind is like so long mind is endless living.

So long, in the mind living is accepted then this place is all of living actor living is it never recognition of macro concept world, or micro concept world or mind level living actor or, wicked soul living actor or truly righteous soul living actor all is not knowing of ignorance living, so then their living is not reach at the righteous soul living of excitement.

Getting much more than others, of mind leveling living actor must be attacked from wicked soul, this is easy living and power of "revenge and break" of wicked soul attack mind level living actor of "getting much more than others" so long wicked soul living actor try to live "easy living" so that wicked soul will get from natural living of ignorance.

What is living? When I felt hard, how to live is excitement living. all of living is so hard, so then I must be" weeping" there is no depend on other, because around of me, I can find righteous soul living actor.

In my work place, I'm an middle manager, then I go with actors who are not know but they are not manners of greeting, they live their living technology, just do work and there is nothing, the relationship is not important but living with working of his job soluble then good.

an actor saying this is my job, so I can do, but this is not related with job so I don't know, this is a point of view is true, but this is righteous soul living point of view is not true, righteous soul living is "it shared time with other, help other, but also doing real love other".

At now I'm writing is hard living me so writing my living is wrong then I feel great, but also I'm sorry, out of me, all of living is not problems all of living is good living.

But truly that is not, all of living actors relationship is bottle, war, there is no peace, how dangerous living, but all is not try to change because here is "endless competition" this is just one of top only one living is winner is living. just one of winner only living all of loser is not care living well or not all is not responsibility endless competition.

Strongly under the endless competition is based on of "righteous soul living of creation of knowledge based, but there is not righteous soul living, but there is wicked soul living, they do not know creation of knowledge, so then wicked soul living actor based of endless competition, so that wicked soul living actor use power of "revenge and break power" so that the place all of living is hard.

With endless competition of fair play then, it must be so good, but do not fair play, but out of fair play is living is "only me easy living" is my living place happening.

In this place, there is Thank you only saying trade, seller saying to the buyer, to sell to make money, but also the best place respected place also in the selling place of alcoholic drinking, so money is power, so long wicked soul living money "easy living" is power because money giving and easy condition getting.

Righteous soul "ME" living in this strong out of righteous soul living, so that my living is hard then I will weep and cry.

I will talk to my god who is king of righteous soul living in destination place.

Voyage 6days

Wicked soul, righteous soul how to affect Righteous soul me in living macro concept world, I got know while writing 8 books.

Macro concept world living natural living actor of ignorance living actors, wicked soul of easy living using power of revenge and breaking others, but also righteous soul living actor of excitement living with doing of "it shared time with other, help other but also doing real love other"

How to executive righteous soul me?

It must be infer that every time and all of situation must be strong affect me then some is wicked soul living actor do breaking so that temptation to me, but also righteous soul living actor help me righteous soul me urgent problems solving.

Recently I got a strong affect me feeling so I want to share what I feeling and wicked soul affect me and righteous soul living actor try to give me solution of my problems.

This is very same as usual day happened, but I felt in the micro concept point "-1/, a Saturday I attended to wedding ceremony for that I use bus to go wedding hale.

Before me a boy and mother seat, then same after, the boy said "I got a two mother, one is living in here, but other is beside seat me, and then the boy anger of saying by the mother, it must be infer of his step mother, she was perplexed.

It occur me why god try to show this scenery to me. This is must be infer that righteous soul me make me learn how to live is right?

In this scenery, why the boy got a two mother, so the boy so sad because of his birth of real mum do not live with him.

A step mother all bear of wrong doer of the boy, she must be boy grown after also being possible hard living with body.

This is result of the boy real mother and father wicked soul living.

Here is righteous soul living god try to learn me is "righteous soul me do live righteously husband and wife, so this living love is so important, this is living all in macro concept world.

The living is righteous soul living actor mission; "bring lover to the righteous soul living in destination place" this is macro concept world righteous soul living actor righteous soul living mission.

If living well with lover then it is normal living, there are no problems, so then all is living in excitement.

Righteous soul me learn that living with lover is so important.

I love my wife; this is so important, righteous soul behavior "it shared time with other, help other and doing real love others" so to the lover is "doing real love is prime living".

Loving is really top priority living, here is my lover is my wife, how to live loving with lover of wife it so important, so that to do "real love", then all of help lover to be righteous soul living.

In the macro concept world, wife and husband living righteous soul living behavior is not carried because they do not know micro concept world righteous soul living actor mission is "bring lover to the righteous soul living in destination place"

If know micro concept world righteous soul living in destination place mission then righteous soul try to do real love lover, all effort, so then, living with lover is so excitement, this is really dream realized before living micro concept world.

At last righteous soul living actor meet lover to bring to the righteous soul living in destination place.

Yes I realized from seeing before seat a boy sad shot, go away to his step mother.

It already a boy father and mother fail to live does real love husband and wife, it is so sad to the boy and his father and mother fail living of righteous soul living actor mission carriage.

Righteous soul living actor tries to teach me, living love with my wife so strong, so that I sent message to my wife "I love you", how important to live loving my wife is now urgent.

Righteous soul living is living well husband and wife, this is righteous soul living. Yes righteous soul living show me in the bus, a strong feeling from boy shouting "do not approach me"

Actually I didn't know why important living righteous soul living doing real love to lover, I see real watching.

Wicked soul me try to "revenge and break", after finish wedding ceremony, turning on my home, I used subway, so then to go for ticketing, so I get on escalator, during going up, then strong affect to me accident occurred to me.

To me seen to me a passenger trouser of back pocket, a smart phone is seen to me, then my wicked soul awaken, thinking is up "stealing smartphone" I was so fear of me, me is stealing it, why that thinking is up, so fear, but also I did not know.

I have smart phone, why wicked soul try to steal thinking, I was so fear, if my behavior followed "thinking of wicked soul" then it must be strong break me, because my macro concept world living all built is broken, it must losing all of my righteous soul living behavior of living "it shared time with other and help other but also doing real love other".

Why "thinking of wicked soul is up to me" truly righteous soul me hasn't anything wanted it, but my "thinking of wicked soul" thinking stealing smartphone.

So scare of this temptation of "thinking of wicked soul", why that kind of wicked soul behavior is occur to me?

At that time I felt, that this is must be before birth living world, I was living of pickpocket, stealer, so that I'm living.

But returning of righteous soul and wicked soul living, yes my wicked soul living actor had lived of pickpocket living, so that the law of inertia, so that righteous soul living actor broken, to do this keep temptation, why seen strongly the back pocket smart phone, so the I was so fear of me.

There am me a pocket picker is living, how to not to do this, this is righteous soul living actor must be give righteous soul of creation of knowledge.

Here is created in the righteous soul living, righteous soul living actor teach "wicked soul living me", this is doing not understood by mind level living actor who understanding is "me" is "natural me" but righteous soul is righteous soul me and wicked soul me is difference in the same body place, body is shelter of wicked soul and righteous soul living actors.

I will teach me, I is righteous soul living actor, but "me" is wicked soul living actor, so that it is so required to me, because of "I" and "ME" is "I" is hurry to safe living and returning to the righteous soul living in destination place, so then "ME" of wicked soul is all the time against to the righteous soul living actor.

So that righteous soul "ME" teach wicked soul living "ME" then there must be create strong righteous soul me of two, then both righteous soul living actor do live in me " it share time with other, and help other but also doing real love other".

In me is forming of righteous soul living in destination place, so long this is very important to do righteous soul living itself is teaching wicked soul living actor in me.

Righteous soul "ME" will teach "wicked soul me", this is comes in this novel.

So long, after retied of my first job then, I will teach me, the righteous soul me teach me, so the tools are video camera and load on the SNS of "you tube" truly I have been fear in the public teaching, but actually I haven't any license in the micro concept world living place teach, so then it required me, righteous soul me is teaching my wicked soul me to be changed to being righteous soul.

So then my teaching is only me, so there are no problems to me, in the macro concept world, my teaching in the public "You Tube".

Every day righteous soul living actor must be hear and see righteous soul living actor teach righteous soul me keep awaken.

Bbut also, wicked soul living actor do keep "temptation to break righteous soul living actor" this is strong "revenge and break".

So then righteous soul living actor keep "awaken" not to be temptation from wicked soul.

But also hear of broadcasting from righteous soul living in destination place.

Voyage 7days

If macro concept world me is living wicked soul, righteous soul, and natural living of mind level living actor what happen to macro concept world "ME" and micro concept world me?

In the macro concept world living actor living ignorance of natural living of mind level living, "getting much more than others" to that all of natural living actor used their time for getting much more than others.

This is time is not used with other of righteous soul living behavior of "it shared time with other, and help other but also doing real love other" natural living actor all of time used for getting much more than others.

In macro concept world natural living actor of mind level living actor to get much more than other, time is not shared with others but also "do not help others" then he must be real of natural living of mind level living actor.

Share time and helping others is not possible of natural living actor of course, busy so that he/she must be doing not real love to lover.

If this living is carried to get much more than others, then the actor reach at the natural living actor of what he/she wanted living?

In this novel key word is "wicked soul", "righteous soul" so long which soul is next appeared up to the natural living actor of mind level living actor.

If a natural living of mind level living actor get much more than other, then a natural living actor dreamed living is permit to him/her to live as rich living.

Truly real world but also in this book "natural of mind level living actor" for getting much more than other, the natural living actor do not living of righteous soul living behavior "it shared time with others, help others, but also doing real love others"

So then getting much more than other natural living actor do not know righteous soul living behavior, all of getting natural living actor follows of money using "easy living", it is natural rich and money is possible in easy living, that is not real living of excitement.

Soon appeared up to the natural of mind level living actor inside is being strong of "wicked soul" of easy living. who knows easy living of wicked soul "easy living" using "revenger and break energy", if a natural living of mind level living actor being changed into wicked soul because wicked soul living actor like to live "easy living" so that wicked soul in the actor keep growing, in a moment all of body occupied by wicked soul.

Wicked soul is master, before natural living of mind level managed me but now wicked soul living actor managed, "easy living actors are collected to new wicked soul living actor.

There is no natural living of mind level, but there is wicked soul living actor so that wicked soul living actor do not know fear, because wicked soul, but natural living actor of mind level living actor know the fear, so that living decision was for the purpose of safe and getting much more than other, but wicked soul is soul, so that the wicked soul living actor decide is only to be "easy living", so that the wicked soul living actor can't go difficult decision living can't living, so that wicked soul decision is do not carry all of variations of living, so long around of wicked soul friends are all seeking "easy living" getting asset used only, so long, there is no function to make asset but only wicked soul living actor can used asset who built natural living of mind level living actor. so lng wicked soul living actor reach at the " breaking wicked soul him/her self".

In this macro concept world if living in righteous soul living then what happened to him/her?

Righteous soul living behavior is "it shared time with others, help other but also doing real love others"

Righteous soul living is appear as mind is about to zero, then greedy mind is living actor disappeared so then appeared to righteous soul living actor.

So long, righteous soul living actor keep go deeper, but also solve hard, difficult problems because to run to the righteous soul living in destination place, so long righteous soul living actor get hear of broadcasting from righteous soul living in destination place, through micro concept tunnel or point "-1/~+1/micro concept is written by me so that if a reader read micro concept book then better to read this book, micro concept book is now selling in amazon.

Righteous soul living actor meet through micro concept tunnel righteous soul in the micro concept world, same doing of righteous soul of macro concept world righteous soul living behavior "it shared time with other and help other but also doing real love others".

So that micro concept world righteous soul tries to do righteous soul behavior to the macro concept world living actors.

Righteous soul living actor living both macro concept world and micro concept world, Righteous soul living actor keep progress such as

Mind disappeared by mind is 1/ this is origin of birth of righteous soul living actor.

Righteous soul living is "the poor & righteous soul living actor" after that "righteous soul & nothing" this is living of righteous soul living.

Righteous soul living actor running for the righteous soul living in destination place, just go with lover, so righteous soul living actor live "it shared time with other, and help other but also doing real love other" righteous soul living actor create living of excitement.

Righteous soul living actor create around of him/her all living actors are living in excitement, because righteous soul living actor sun bright energy is spread around of righteous soul living.

How good around of righteous soul living actors, so long, which living is create excitement with others, so then it required to live in righteous soul living.

If an macro concept world as righteous soul living then how feel excitement with around of me, all of me is righteous soul living or not, all is from me, but not others living in excitement.

Voyage 8days

What I did book writing, selling books are in the amazon. Perfectly nothing selling in the market, this is also pushing me to writing in excitement.

Truly book writing is based on excitement so then book selling is not matter to me but to the amazon marketing problems, my living is not depend on book selling.

Truly this is real and righteous soul, but wicked soul living actor me is expecting selling books in the market.

My time consuming is writing this is really excitement living, but book writing is affect from against to my writing, sometimes writing creation of knowledge tunnel is blocked, this is must be against me of wicked soul behavior of "revenge and break".

What is living? Living is consuming times. But living is production living energy. Consuming energy is time is used for "easy living" of wicked soul living, but production energy is righteous soul behavior "it shared time with other and help other, but also doing real love other".

Righteous soul living is macro and micro concept world cycle living. Start from righteous soul living in destination place with getting real love other energy to macro concept world living doing "it shard time with others, and help others, and doing real love others". Ultimate bring lover to the righteous soul living in destination place.

This is righteous soul living actor excitement road. Hear is righteous living actor road is running to the righteous soul living in destination place.

Infer that it is similar of macro concept world "Tao" this is living righteous soul living, but also "enlighten living".

But so hard to live in "running to the righteous soul living in destination place" because "easy living of wicked soul" is temptation from wicked souls.

Running to the righteous soul living in destination place, then righteous soul living actor "the poor & righteous soul living" would be temptation of "easy living of wicked soul", most living in macro concept world to live "easy living try to living getting much more than other of mind level living of nature living".

How to live in excitement? Where feeling excitement? Micro concept world in me feeing, micro concept world is strong segregated righteous soul from wicked soul living in destination place.

Righteous soul living is feeling of "excitement" wicked soul living feeling is "easy living". Here is righteous soul of "excitement" is included in the poor living, but wicked soul of "easy living" is not included in "the poor living".

Truly these days macro concept world living "me" is doing not feeling in excitement. To live excitement is try to be "mind is about to zero, and the poor and righteous soul, righteous soul & nothing" this is real me.

Writing is feeling in "excitement", writing is helped from righteous soul living furthermore, righteous soul living in destination place keep broadcasting to the righteous soul living actors, to run for the righteous soul living in destination place helping safe returning to the righteous soul living in destination place.

This is only feeling hearing broadcasting from righteous soul living in destination place.

What is safe returning to the righteous soul living in destination place? in the living in micro concept world they lived in so excitement in the righteous soul living in destination place, but a righteous soul living actor to do mission carry start macro concept world voyage then, safe returning righteous soul living actor know that how hard to returning to the righteous soul living in destination place, so that righteous soul living actor feeling is try to help voyage to macro concept world "doing real love energy" because all of hard living endure only doing "real love other".

"Real love other energy" is used with wicked soul living. All of time in the macro concept world, then mostly natural living actor and wicked soul living actors are front line, so that righteous soul living actor buffer zone making is "using energy of real love other" then directly damage is not to righteous soul living.

"Real love other energy" is also created and produced from righteous soul living itself is energy generator, but also helped from righteous soul living in destination place through micro concept tunnel or point(-1/ : micro concept ;seong ju choi), then righteous soul living actor being excitement feeling.

Excitement feeling is affected from micro concept world or macro concept world, micro concept world is feeling, but macro concept world is seeing.

Macro concept world seeing is just like micro concept point, the same as broadcasting to micro concept world, this is really excitement just like see "rose flower" then it must be excitement is from seeing rose flowers, the moment this rose flower broadcasting to the micro concept world living actors.

But feeling in excitement is from micro concept world, micro concept world righteous soul living actors are try to do behavior of righteous soul living "it shard time with other, help other but also doing real love other" so that micro concept world righteous soul do behavior of righteous soul to the macro concept world righteous soul living actor, so then macro concept world righteous soul living actor through micro concept point hearing and feeling excitement and creation of righteous knowledge.

Creation of knowledge is only from righteous soul living in destination place through righteous soul micro concept point. here is infer that all of macro concept world righteous soul living problems are all solved from righteous soul living actors hearing and feeling from righteous soul living in destination place broadcasting.

Excitement living is these process is required, but in the living of macro concept world, all of hard with natural living actor and wicked soul living actors then do tumble down to the ground.

Righteous soul living actor so hard to live with natural living actors getting much more than others, but also wicked soul doing power of "revenge and break" so that righteous soul living actor affected deep hard living such as variable stress in the macro concept world.

In this time righteous soul must keep awaken then it must be helped from righteous soul living in destination place, because of righteous soul living actor excitement is based on righteous soul helping and doing real love.

Righteous soul living is so feeble with natural living actor and wicked soul living actor, so that righteous soul living actor being just like "monk water" "losing gamer" of my nick name, because fighting getting quarrel is not win, but the power depend on helping from righteous soul living in destination place.

Righteous soul living is so strong in the righteous soul living actor all is doing each other "it shared time with other, help other but also doing real love others", if a place all living actor is nature living actor and wicked soul living actor remove all of righteous soul living actor then, who will be role of the poor and losing gamer but also monk water of lowest place living, then it must be there is defunct righteous soul of "creation of knowledge", but there is no lowest position of losing gamer role player is not there so that, naturally the place is wicked soul and natural living of mind level living actor conflict happened. Then the place is all is hell.

How to live? It is righteous soul living behavior is so living; living itself is righteous soul living behavior of "the poor & righteous soul" and "righteous soul & nothing. This is heling peace in the macro concept world.

To live peace in the macro concept world is so required to the righteous soul living actor, so that it undertake role of the lowest place living, so that my nick name is "monk water" and "losing gamer" of living in excitement.

"Monk water" and "losing gamer" is living of righteous soul living "me" this living is so hard, but there is no way, because my living is so feeble, so that rather I do not quarrel to win in position so I usually living in the lowest living.

My work place promotion game all ruined but strange I'm now positioning I'm satisfying now, even hard living to live in this place all of quarrel was lose but now survive, how to live now is it must be other righteous soul living actor behavior "it shared time with other and help other but also doing real love other" so that a someplace righteous soul living actor do behavior of righteous soul so that I'm here.

You know! The poor & righteous soul is so strong. I'm living in the circle in the righteous soul living actors so I'm in excitement living every time and place.

Voyage 9days

Creation of knowledge from righteous soul living in destination place is to help righteous soul living actor running to righteous soul living in destination place.

Macro concept world living actor live to get much more than others, so this is competition winning, this is knowledge. So long natural living actor of mind level living actor depend on knowledge, so long macro concept world mind level living actor of natural living actor knowledge is "to get much more than other" here other is all of out of me.

But Creature of knowledge from righteous soul living in destination place through "micro concept point, tunnel", this is to help righteous soul living actor running safe for the righteous soul living destination reaching.

Here is Creation of knowledge is getting by hearing broadcasting from righteous soul living in destination place.

What is micro concept point is "-1/~+1/ micro concept point is derived from "book of micro concept; seong ju Choi", wicked soul living actor living in the -/0 ~-1/, but righteous soul living actor is living +1/~+/0.

So long micro concept point of "-1/∞~+1/∞" creation of knowledge getting tunnel and point.

Wicked soul living actor is only -1/, but righteous soul living actor is +1/, knowledge is connect already built knowledge and next building knowledge so that micro concept point is tunnel of creation of knowledge getting. It must be inferred of spring of cleaning water, changed saying of creature of knowledge.

In the natural living actor place, who is winner is mostly to solve the examination then this knowledge is already built knowledge. so long, all of living actor in the macro concept living actor, for the purpose of easy living, most try to learn already existed knowledge.

This knowledge is possible test that is getting well or not, so long this test points are lead to the ranking.

All of macro concept world living actor knowledge is power to open the what he/she want to do, their living way to support hem/her.

So long they all do not care to be building creation of knowledge. Creation of knowledge is to be get so hard living, because of righteous soul living actor behavior is "it shared time with other, and doing help other, but also do real love other", this is not living of natural living of getting much more than others.

Here is very important thing is occurring, to live easy, just all cling to the already built knowledge learning then the place is must be do not go into creation of knowledge, then in the end all of knowledge is too old to old knowledge is useless knowledge, so then the place is being deteriorate.

So long, the place living actors are all living of wicked soul living behavior of "revenge and break" in the end the place all be broken.

But Creation of knowledge bring a righteous soul living actor whose living is "it shard time with other, and help other but also doing real love other", their living is depend on creation of knowledge derived from micro concept point, tunnel of -1/~+1/.

Righteous soul living actor living from "the poor & righteous soul" it growing to "righteous soul & nothing" so that righteous soul living actor living so hard living, but the living runs to the righteous soul living in destination place.

Righteous soul living actor knowledge from righteous soul living in destination place, this creation of knowledge is hearing broadcasting from righteous soul living in destination place.

So long, in the macro concept world, natural living of mind level living actor depend on already built knowledge but in the living of righteous soul living actor place is depend on creation of knowledge from righteous soul living in destination place.

In the end natural living actor use knowledge and righteous soul living actor use Creation of knowledge, even living in the macro concept world but using knowledge is not same, difference.

Creation of knowledge using righteous soul living actor living in eternity but already built knowledge user of wicked soul living actor do not live in eternity.

How to discriminate whose living was righteous soul living or wicked soul living are difference because wicked soul living of living of already built living knowledge depend on living actor being disappeared since he/she dead, but if an actor live in creation of knowledge of righteous soul living then, after dead, his/her of righteous soul living using knowledge living eternity after all of natural living actor use his/her creation of knowledge.

In the living feeling, all of knowledge used for me, here is me is same but if knowledge is from already built knowledge to teach "me" then "ME" is not grow to the future but, "ME" is taught from creation of knowledge then "ME" is keep grown to the righteous soul living "ME", so then creation of knowledge is eternity living of righteous soul living in destination place arriving.

"ME" of righteous soul living actor is changed natural living, or wicked soul living "ME" is changed through learn of creation knowledge from righteous soul living in destination place, through micro concept point, hearing broadcasting from righteous soul living in destination place.

Original righteous soul living actor purpose is to teach "ME" of wicked soul or natural living of mind level living actor. So long original righteous soul living actor must be awaken to hear of broadcasting from righteous soul living in destination place.

Then original righteous soul hearing creation of knowledge and teach "ME" of wicked soul, natural living of mind level living actor to be changed into righteous soul "ME".

Why original righteous soul living actor do awaken is here saying, "ME" changed into righteous soul living. After this original righteous soul living actor safe living and returning to the righteous soul living in destination place.

Because safe returning righteous soul living actor keep growing because a living of macro concept world living actor soul room "righteous soul with doing real love and wicked soul of "revenge and break" so that original righteous soul keep hearing broadcasting from righteous soul living, so that original righteous soul living actor to the wicked soul "ME" do live righteous soul living behavior of "it shared time with wicked soul, but also help wicked soul, and in the and do real love wicked soul" so then use teach "wicked soul me using creation of knowledge from righteous soul living in destination place.

So that wicked soul changed into righteous soul living enough and perfect righteous soul to live in righteous soul living in destination place. Perfect righteous soul "ME" is strong righteous soul living, so that in the living of righteous soul "ME" also keep do broadcasting now coming to righteous soul living actor running to the righteous soul living in destination place.

Safe returning to the righteous soul living in destination place, the actor living is so excitement living in the righteous soul living in destitution place in eternity.

Voyage 10days

I'm running to the righteous soul living in destination place. Who will make block the way to the righteous soul me going righteous soul living in destination place?

Living is breath oxygen and keep drive me safe and running righteous soul living in destination place.

Here is keep drive is momentum decision, living in the macro concept world living actor must be live in "decision with breath" all of living is micro concept world and macro concept world is connected living.

Micro concept world living is "start righteous soul living destination place to voyage macro concept world to get lover to the micro concept world righteous soul living in destination place.

Macro concept world living support body hunger so that body living safe so that follow "mind" "mind ordered macro concept me to live perfect safe you getting much more than others" so Macro concept world hurry to do it.

If macro concept world living actor living focus for "body safe with keeping mind order getting much more than others" this is macro concept world or mind level living actor must be not wrong.

But there is micro concept world living also "bring lover to the righteous soul living in destination place.

Micro concept world living of righteous soul living actor do follows doing mission clear, this is so important righteous soul living in eternity living with lover is why righteous soul living actor start voyage to the macro concept world.

Righteous soul in the macro concept world living actor running for the righteous soul living in destination place, not lost read to righteous soul living in destination place.

Righteous soul living actor running to the righteous soul living in destination place! it must be not an structure but not an structure; not seen but also can't describe it.

it must be inferring that righteous soul living actor running to the righteous soul living must be keeping open and closed gate going or not, so then here is keep open in the righteous soul living actor then it must be strong righteous soul living energy to go through.

But righteous soul living actor energy is losing then it must hard to go through running to the righteous soul living in destination place.

Righteous soul running to the righteous soul living in destination place is required of doing behavior of righteous soul living "it shared time with other, help other but also doing real love other" and safe living with wicked soul living actor, and it must hearing broadcasting from righteous soul living in destination place so called "creation of knowledge".

Righteous soul living is energy is getting doing living of righteous soul living behavior and safe living with wicked soul, it must do using "real love others" doing real love wicked soul make wicked soul to righteous soul living actor.

Righteous soul living all of problems are happened so then, it must be required to live knowledge, so then "creation of knowledge" is helping righteous soul living actor living in the macro concept world.

just righteous soul living actor live hard and poor living because in the macro concept world living place, mind level living actor try to live "easy living" but also mind level living actor "getting much more than others" so that righteous soul living actor of "it shared time with other, help other but also doing real love other", so that it is real of hard living is clear.

Running to the righteous soul living in destination place is micro concept world living actor urgent living, righteous soul living actor's living all, prime living this living is so excitement living but also reach at righteous soul living is real living, other is all dead, so that to live in real living righteous soul living must be keep running in the road to righteous soul living in destination place.

Voyage 11days

Wicked souls want to live in "easy living" to easy living wicked soul use living energy "revenge and break".

Wicked soul living actor really to live easy living is living purpose so that their target is natural living actor of follow of mind, so that all of living is getting much more than others, so then if natural living actor endless to get from other all of time consuming, then in the end wanting to live easy living of wicked soul principle in break the reach at the peak of the getting much more than others.

The natural living actor hurry living follow of mind, so then mind is "getting much more than others" is mind level living actor living rule, so that natural living of mind level then the natural living actor all time is used up gathering asset, but also busy collecting asset so that they have not time to help other, so long so busy getting asset so mind level living actor do not real love others.

The peak of getting natural living actor then natural living actor feel be "happy of rich living" but awaiting wicked soul living actor use "revenge and break" so that peak natural living actor living in the wicked soul living actors place.

Micro concept world, peak of rich living actor righteous soul living actor almost dead, then wicked soul is so strong in the end natural living actor already changed into wicked soul living actor.

Macro concept world, natural living actor of following mind, so that the natural living actor all get his/her living without living of righteous soul living behavior "it shard time with other, help other but also doing real love other".

So that peak in natural living actor living actor of micro and macro concept world there are any righteous soul living actor of energies.

This living actor of natural living actor in principle is attacked from wicked soul living actor to live easy living by using "revenge and break".

So that to be rich and happy but the living in wicked soul and around of him/her all are wicked soul, so that all of living is "revenge and break" in the end of natural living changed into wicked soul living actor, so that all of easy living by using money. As that wicked soul living perfectly forgot to get righteous soul living energy. Their living all is consuming time consuming, and asset consuming furthermore all segregate from money stolen fear so that they are segregated from closed relatives also.

Wicked soul living actor living world where are macro concept world and micro concept world.

Micro concept world is righteous soul living in the righteous soul living in destination place, and then there is no wicked soul because of righteous soul living actor living in righteous soul living in destination place.

But Righteous soul living actor run for the macro concept world then, after voyage then wicked soul also to revenge and break run out to macro concept world, then wicked soul living actor is getting with righteous soul living actor, so then righteous soul living actor purpose to voyage to macro concept world then even mission in the macro concept world is not same, righteous soul living actor getting energy of "doing real love other to lover bring back to the righteous soul living in destination place" but wicked soul living actor is anger of why living in the wicked soul so that to do "revenge and break" so why tour in the macro concept world living place is not same.

Macro concept world wicked soul living actor try to live in easy living so that they use "revenge and break energy" wicked soul living actor go with mind is full of living actor, so that wicked soul living actor mindful living actor who are living damaged other but also to get other be hard, so long, they are might be target of wicked soul living actor's "revenge and breaking".

But righteous soul living actor macro concept world living purpose is meet lover then" safe bring righteous soul making and lover bring back to the righteous soul living in destination place".

This is macro concept world living, at now I'm writing so that I know that there are livings; wicked souls and mind level living actors but also expect to live with righteous soul living actors.

As my living, I feel fear of wicked soul living actor "revenge me and break me" sometimes I felt so fear, because of wicked soul living actor energy strong to me, if trying to be living in righteous soul living me, as getting being strong righteous soul, then strong wicked soul always with me.

Truly wicked soul, righteous soul is same "ME", in me is macro concept world and micro concept world, so that what explained that in me, righteous soul living actor and wicked soul living actor is same living.

Wicked soul living me is keep doing " revenge and break me" this is so fear to me, wicked soul living actor impulse to steal other, but also sometimes wicked soul living actor keep damage me how to know if some of reading this book.

I see in me, happening in me wicked soul living actor behavior and righteous soul living behavior is like this.

Wicked soul living actor macro concept world connect is "thinking of wicked soul" but righteous soul living behavior is "broadcasting from righteous soul living in destination place".

"Thinking of wicked soul" is based on to live "easy living" all of other getting removal others, here is other is "ME" if my righteous soul living try to live in "the poor & righteous soul living" then strongly against to the righteous soul living behavior.

So long, righteous soul living behavior of "the poor & righteous soul living" attacked from "thinking of wicked soul" try to live "easy living".

Wicked soul living in the macro concept world to live "easy living" the fear of other living making hard using "revenge and break" so then here I will not saying whoever know what happened in the macro concept world.

How to live? This is urgent living question! But truly all of macro concept world living me still do not find how to live? I do not answer still.

It is not with living with wicked soul living! How to out of wicked soul living, whoever else all I will live in righteous soul living, then truly righteous soul living must be needed to enlighten so then how to live enlighten, this is real living, so that how to live to the answer is "living in enlighten living". This is macro concept world living actor's forerunners living this way.

In this book, to be living in righteous soul living then, righteous soul living actor living is hard then easy living of wicked soul getting distance so then, righteous soul living energy must be strong then, wicked soul living actor also be possible by strong righteous soul living actor" doing real love wicked soul" then it is real living this is how to live? Solving the problems is living in righteous soul living.

Voyage 12days

In my living "ME" every moment pushed to me time and space of "thinking of wicked soul" and then if broken pushing up of "thinking of wicked soul" then just a short of moment hearing of righteous soul living broadcasting to help coming to righteous soul living in destination place.

Truly micro concept world "wicked soul living" "righteous soul living" is in the micro concept world "ME", I have been believed until now.

But today some of eccentric creation of knowledge from righteous soul living in destination place, the creation of knowledge is "righteous soul "ME" living out of thinking of wicked soul".

Righteous soul living actor voyage from righteous soul living in destination place, as meet body then righteous soul living actor get in to problems of mind, so that mind is naturally consist of "me" recognition is "righteous soul + mind + body" this is me of natural living of righteous soul living possible when mind is 1/,

Then it must be "righteous soul + body" then truly righteous soul is unseen world living actor so that actually "righteous soul & nothing" so then it must be "body" only, so long, as mind is getting about to zero then righteous soul is position at instead of mind so long " righteous soul + body" being righteous soul living.

"ME" is truly righteous soul, so "righteous soul & nothing" if this then living only righteous soul living, but here is important is done of righteous soul living, where remained after being righteous soul living.

This is so important, because being "righteous soul & nothing" is so moment, so that to be eternity living in "righteous soul & nothing" then it must be segregated from wicked soul.

Wicked soul is understand in the macro concept world as "thinking of wicked soul" so that wicked soul =thinking, wicked soul living express through thinking, so wicked soul living actor live in the past, wicked soul living actor mission is before living do harmed to living at wicked soul living in destination place suffer living, so that wicked soul living actor keep "revenge and break" this is wicked soul living actor mission.

Thinking of wicked soul start from past did, at now pay before damaged to "ME" so that wicked soul "ME" pushed in me as the form of "thinking of wicked soul"

Righteous soul living actor hears of broadcasting from righteous soul living in destination place, so that this broadcasting hearing is creation of knowledge from the future.

So long, in "ME" try to give me, through broadcasting is give "creation of knowledge" but wicked soul living through "thinking of wicked soul" "keep make me "revenge and break", so long truly righteous soul "ME" and wicked soul "ME" is same information getting.

Wicked soul is getting information from wicked soul living in destination past what did, so that revenge and break other.

Righteous soul is getting information from righteous soul living in destination place future what does, so "it shared time with other, help other and doing real love other".

Truly micro concept world living is segregated from wicked soul living of past living place, righteous soul living is living in the future living place.

If righteous soul living actor safe living in the macro concept world living then, the righteous soul living actor run to the future of righteous soul living in destination place, so that starting time righteous soul living in destination place much more future of righteous soul living in destination place safe returning.

So long the righteous soul living actor is keep growing for fitting future living world.

In the micro concept world wicked soul and righteous soul living actor segregated so that righteous soul living actor "it shared time with other, help other but also doing real love other", but wicked soul living actor living in the wicked soul living in destination place, "wicked soul do revenge and break each other".

So that righteous soul living actor do not difficult living from wicked soul in the macro concept world living.

But truly macro concept world righteous soul living actor lives so hard from thinking of wicked soul, "anger, fear, and frustrate hunger. Etc.

Thinking of wicked soul is reminding "ME" may be forgotten to be absolutely "do revenge and break" so that living of righteous soul living actor so hard living awaken of wicked soul behavior.

So that righteous soul living actor remained at out of thinking of wicked soul, where truly living in the macro concept world, righteous soul living actor place is not damaged thinking of wicked soul, so that every turning damaged to righteous soul, so that truly distance from wicked soul just like micro concept world segregated from wicked soul.

In the macro concept world righteous soul "ME" living out of wicked soul "ME", it is possible because righteous soul is "righteous soul & nothing" already, there is no living anyplace but just feeling of righteous soul living.

Macro concept world, it must be keep arising "thinking of wicked soul" so then I will not follows of thinking of wicked soul information, so long it must be live in righteous soul living keep hearing righteous soul living in destination place broadcasting.

Voyage 13days

Wicked soul how to feel? Wicked soul is "thinking of wicked soul" wicked soul push up into thinking tunnel of past information. "Thinking of wicked soul" keep make reminding of past anger to do "revenge and breaking other".

This is so fear of it, "thinking of wicked soul" do "revenge me and break me" this is so fear to the righteous soul living actor.

"Thinking of wicked soul" is changing come and disappeared, so that "thinking of wicked soul" is drift in the righteous soul traveling place, sometimes cloudy of "thinking of wicked soul" is coming.

Righteous soul living actor just see "thinking of wicked soul cloudy" if this cloudy sometimes rains, snow, wind etc.

"Thinking of wicked soul" just cloud come and see, so that if "thinking of wicked soul" disappeared then the place is clean sky of the righteous soul feel excitement in the body of world.

Truly macro concept world living actor all occur of "thinking of wicked soul" some of sensible actor will see what happened in the body world, not out of body, in the place without control of anger wiliness comes.

Drift cloudy of Thinking of wicked soul just limited in past, so that all of "thinking of wicked soul typhoon" role of same as wicked soul of "revenge and break others" so then "thinking of wicked soul typhoon" powerful anger to me and others, in this case righteous soul living actor so fear, somewhat righteous soul would be damaged to be disappeared from running to the righteous soul living in destination place.

This is righteous soul do not safe returning to the righteous soul living in destination place.

"Thinking of wicked soul" strong "revenge and break" do harm in macro concept world include "me", truly in the natural phenomenon, all of accident is from "thinking of wicked soul" but most macro concept world accident is not me but others, but all of accident is directly from me, so then, "thinking of wicked soul" use me to do "revenge and break" others, in this happening damaged me and others.

So that the poor & righteous soul is living poor, this is wicked soul try to live in "easy living" so that "hard living" hate, so long, this is explained in the natural living but truly in micro concept then hard to explain in writing.

Righteous soul know that "thinking of wicked soul" is not helpful living of righteous soul so that righteous soul prepare of "thinking of wicked soul cloudy" depend just watch not cling to the "thinking of wicked soul" but in the natural living, then an actor of macro concept world, anger then, righteous soul actor also included in the "thinking of wicked soul cloudy" so that in the body world, all be "thinking of wicked soul cloudy" there were not sunshine of clean weather.

So long, in the body world all be in "thinking of wicked soul world" so that strong wicked soul living energy, just time all living of wicked soul living.

In this time righteous soul living actor disappeared, so that naturally do wicked soul living behavior "revenge and break including me and other"

Thinking of wicked soul use "me" revenge and break other, what happen to me, in the macro concept world I'm being wrong doer to other, in the end "ME" living is deteriorate so long, "ME" of righteous soul living target of breaking, this is not other but "me of thinking of wicked soul".

damage me breaking me from "thinking of wicked soul" then truly in the body difference me and other is living, but here is me is righteous soul living actor is real me, so that righteous soul living actor run for the righteous soul living in destination place so that so urgent to live in righteous soul living "it shard time with other, and helping other but also doing real love other"

Righteous soul living actor do live in righteous soul living, but hardly the other me of wicked soul "ME" is truly enemy to the righteous soul living actor.

So that living in the macro concept world, is result of micro concept world coming out, righteous soul living is giving "true of creature of knowledge" this is helping righteous soul living actor running to the righteous soul living in destination place.

This "truth of creature of knowledge" and "thinking of wicked soul" is difference strongly, macro concept actor living body is brains of head so that occur to the head in the natural living generally thinking but this is it can't express "truth of creature of knowledge" this is righteous soul living tunnel, my book "micro concept" then micro concept tunnel, meet macro concept actor righteous soul meet micro concept righteous soul to solve macro concept actor of righteous soul running to the righteous soul living in destination place.

So then, natural living actor does not discrimination between "thinking of wicked soul and "truth of creature of knowledge" but micro concept world clear of difference gate, tunnel.

Wicked soul is "thinking of wicked soul" please this book readers see "thinking is only related with past, but "truth of creature of righteous soul" is related with future, so that righteous soul living "truth of creature of righteous soul" is creature of solving, so that it can be possible of righteous soul running to the righteous soul living.

What is righteous soul living? Actually in this natural living, it is not easy, an actor living is not four directions south, west, north east, in a time an actor chose a direction, then truly open for one direction, to get through a direction it must be required to solve problems, so then, If not solve problems, the actor living is prisoning past living.

This is naturally strong related with "thinking of wicked soul" so then closed living actor just go around in the past knowledge living.

This actor do not getting from righteous soul living actor of micro concept world, so that wicked soul living actor only used righteous soul living actor used knowledge.

Truly very well past knowledge then past knowledge information used place living well, truly the living actor can't do righteous soul living behavior "it shared time with other, help other but also doing real love other", just old knowledge based living actor living is closed related living of "thinking of wicked soul' each other revenge and break.

But righteous soul of "truth of creature of knowledge" is coming now running time getting knowledge, so that it must be, righteous soul living actor open east, south west, north 4 directions, so that get through the gate, so keep running for the future and righteous soul living in destination place.

How to appeared in the macro concept world, then an actor living of righteous soul living is living well with others but also their living also going well, but wicked soul of past living actor, is red ocean it must be, the place is not clean but dirty, just like from well fresh water of creation of knowledge, but the water run to down, then all of old materials are melting in the water, so then the water is not pure, the water mixed with dirty, in the end the water is not creation of knowledge not any more but the knowledge is old knowledge with deceit or wicked soul living, "revenge and break other".

Truly long river and reach at the sea, the old salty water evaporated to the heaven and downfall to the ground, this is living, but if old knowledge living actor blocking circulation because of old knowledge at first getting is prime living. so from wall clean water to be wall clean water being is longer.

Wicked soul living actor is wicked soul cloudy then, if cloudy weather is regard as real living then, the place is not follows of real righteous soul of clear of sunshine, then cloudy living actor argue is this past knowledge is true, then bright sunshine time creature of knowledge is not accepted then the place must be try to be keep under living of cloudy weather living.

Wicked soul living truly their living is not wrong, but the living is old, but also they the old living knowledge can't solve now problems, this problems is running for the out of before past to future so that, they can't go for the future.

But wicked soul living actors are all strong believe in old knowledge, at now coming knowledge is not accepted. because wicked soul living is "easy living" so that getting in the strong power living of wicked souls are there is no problems even understructure is broken, because their old knowledge living actor, try to used so called truth, but that can't solve now problems.

Cloudy living wicked soul living actor do not accept bright of new creature of knowledge.

Wicked soul how to feel? is "thinking of wicked soul" is keep cling to the past accident making remember to "revenge and break", but also "thinking of wicked soul" is living in past, so that past is old knowledge living who does not accept "creation of knowledge from righteous soul living in destination place" then it is wicked soul living feeling.

Voyage 14days

"Thinking of wicked soul" is talking on "easy living" "revenge and break other", wicked soul living actor talking useless all the day in the macro concept world.

So that righteous soul living actor hearing all of "thinking of wicked soul" talking is all chatter.

Righteous soul living actor talking is related with "it shared time with other, helping other and doing real love other"

"Thinking of wicked soul" talking, "easy living" talking is to make easy money, to be living rich to be easy living, "easy living" do not know hard living excitement. "Easy living" talking is "body health living to live in longer than others"

Body strong with easy living is all of wicked soul living actor common talking; this is so good to the easy living actors to make hidden essential real living, so that "easy living is strong related with chattering.

"Thinking of wicked soul" strong related with "revenge and break other" wicked soul living actor talking is anger or curse word, deceit word, it may be deceit is also "easy living" wicked soul living actor.

It must be true, all the day talking, macro concept world living actor talking is world all related with "easy living" "revenge and break".

"Thinking of wicked soul" is so closed to the righteous soul living actor, so that "Thinking of wicked soul" talking is effecting on righteous soul living peace living.

"Wicked soul" and "righteous soul" is not same living in the micro concept world, so that "wicked soul" living style and "righteous soul" living style is not same.

In the micro concept world, wicked soul living in destination place, their living is natural living of only me easy living and to be easy living do revenge and break others.

But micro concept world of righteous soul living in destination place, the place living actors are "it shared time with other, help other, but also doing real love other"

Therefore living in the macro concept world, mine level living actor whose do not know existing righteous soul, wicked soul, and wicked soul living and righteous soul living actors are living in the same place, truly do not know who is mind level living actor, or wicked soul living actor but also righteous soul living actor.

So that righteous soul living actor is "righteous soul living "ME", righteous soul living actor run for the righteous soul living in destination place.

Righteous soul living actor did enlighten so that it understand how to live is righteous soul living, so that righteous soul living actor has trying to help other, but that is most related with "wicked soul, mind level living actor, but also other righteous souls"

That is righteous soul living actor contaminated from wicked soul living actors, so that righteous soul living actor would be damaged running to the righteous soul living in destination place.

The scar of damage somehow righteous soul living running road must be broken so out of road, so that righteous soul living actor feeling is losing enlightenment.

Enlightened righteous soul "ME" living in so small living, whoever despise me but there is accepted all of wicked soul, mind level living actor indicate me, my small living.

Small living is me, "righteous soul "ME" then living in the narrow wide and deep in the indefinite because all of "getting much more than others of mind level living actor conflict, but also wicked soul stealth mind level living actor getting assets, so righteous soul living "me" to live in righteous soul living "me" living time and space is micro concept point (-1/ ~ +1/) only.

Small living "me" righteous soul "me" then, the time and space is micro concept point, there it never effect from wicked soul and mind level living actor, small living of righteous soul living is living in the micro concept point(-1/∞ ~ +1/∞).

Righteous soul, "mall living" is also challenge to me, but righteous soul "ME" is living small is all enduring of hard living. it must be "small me is segregated from wicked soul, and mind level living actor.

How to live in small living, truly this is micro concept of principle, small living of righteous soul "Me" can be possible to live in excitement, there is no excitement between living of righteous soul but living in wicked soul, mind level living, righteous soul "ME" must be living in righteous soul, there also feeling in excitement.

"Thinking of wicked soul" chattering, they do not talk truth, all of "thinking of wicked soul" talking of useless to live true living, but all are chattering only, these talking any helping righteous soul living actor running for the righteous soul living in destination place.

Here is can't express by word, "wicked soul and righteous soul in the soul room" this is what I can't explain but true, so that this is living of the micro and macro mixed hybrid living, place, this is correlated with each other, if "me" is in the wicked soul then suffer from wicked soul to righteous soul "ME", but if I be live in righteous soul living then, hybrid "me" is feel excitement of righteous soul me, at that time it must be infer that of wicked soul living actor power of "revenge and break" energy must be decreased.

All be understand but also righteous soul "me" do explain in the macro concept world, wicked soul living actor, mind level living actor, righteous soul living actor, this is complicate to make it clear, because all of living actor in the natural living macro concept world, they are living, they all has same structure of righteous soul, wicked soul, but also mind level living actor.

How to discriminate it is not easy, righteous soul living actor do not segregate all is same in the righteous soul living. it must be wicked soul living actor can be segregate from righteous soul living actor.

Because "Easy living wicked soul" used "revenge and break" then who will be target is " righteous soul living actor", so that righteous soul living actor must be living "small living" then "small living" actor it don't have to use their " revenge and break power" so righteous soul "ME" living small living, so called "the poor & righteous soul living".

"Small living" is how to living? It must do not expand just live in micro concept point $(-1/\infty \sim +1/\infty)$.

Even righteous soul "me" know because I wrote book "micro concept" if reading in this book, please read "micro concept".

I can live in micro concept point.

Voyage 15days

Wicked soul keep doing "revenge & breaking" righteous soul "ME", Righteous soul living actor growing means that wicked soul do not see "righteous soul me", then safe from wicked soul "revenge and breaking" righteous soul "ME"

Righteous soul living actor keep running to the righteous soul living in destination place, further more righteous soul living actor keep lighter in the end do not seen to the wicked soul living actor.

Wicked soul living actor tries to get heavier as growing, so that try to be living in "easy living". Wicked soul living actor prime aiming is to live "easy living". to be easy living other must be living hard living, so that wicked soul living actor offend other.

Wicked soul living actor to be live easy living offends other wicked soul then, the place happened serious accident.

Wicked soul offend to righteous soul living then, righteous soul living actor do real love wicked soul, so that the place, righteous soul living actor hard living. but righteous soul living oneself does by ones decision, so that that was also still running to the righteous soul living in destination place.

Righteous soul living actor running for the righteous soul living in destination place, then it required to the righteous soul producing creating new energy full covering running to the righteous soul living in destination place.

Wicked soul living actor bans to do creating righteous soul living actor energy getting. Then if same as wicked soul as running to get full, righteous soul living actor all disappeared running for the righteous soul living in destination place.

Truly infer of righteous soul living actor getting poor, " it shared time with others, help other, but also doing real love other" then the righteous soul living actor all used up of wicked soul living actor what it want to get.

So long, the poor & righteous soul living actor, it must be explained as the poor of mind and being righteous soul living, this is understood from natural living of mind level living actor getting much more than others, so that as do not getting much more than other, wicked soul living actor being all used up wicked soul energy, so then, righteous soul living actor energy only for using running traveling for the righteous soul living in destination place.

If righteous soul living actor reach at the "righteous soul & nothing" then even righteous soul, but in the book to differentiation from the poor and righteous soul living, truly the poor is only in the mind level living place, because wicked soul living actor all get to be easy living then, lower of righteous soul living actor living in righteous soul living, but in the righteous soul living in destination place, there is no "the poor", just only living in righteous soul living actor only, truly there all "righteous soul".

It must be righteous soul living in destination place living actor is only "soul" because, in the righteous soul living place, do not know existence of "wicked soul" so that, righteous soul living in destination place is truly real of living.

As growing righteous soul living actor, so called running to the righteous soul living in destination place, all of wicked soul living actors are all disturb righteous soul living actor running to the righteous soul living in destination place.

In the macro concept world, variable living actors are mixed living such as righteous soul living actor, wicked soul living actor, mind level living actor, so then all of living actor meet each other then, righteous soul living actor closed living actors are army of wicked soul and mind level living actors.

Keep supplied to the wicked soul and mind level living actor, obstruct righteous soul living actor running for the righteous soul living in destination place.

So why righteous soul living actor run safe not to be trouble from wicked soul and mind level living actor.

Macro concept world, lover makes righteous soul "me" so hard, but at this time must be use for creating righteous soul living in destination running energy.

If lover endless trouble then do real love lover, it is mission righteous soul living actor living, lover still strong wicked soul, so righteous soul "ME" living is so hard, but "righteous soul "ME" keep doing real love lover then, the lover must be changed from wicked soul to righteous soul, this is righteous soul living actor creating energy, creating energy is doing real love, and help other, but also doing time live with other.

If do not then, righteous soul living actor energy must be used up, so then, even righteous soul living actor being enlighten but soon energy used up, then faced to the strong wicked soul, in the end, righteous soul living actor also disappeared in the end living only wicked soul living.

In a moment, a righteous soul living actor out of running way to the righteous soul living in destination place.

Truly righteous soul "me" is real living, but all of wicked soul living and mind level living of getting much more than other is all is circumstance, so called stages of righteous soul living actor running to the righteous soul living in destination place.

If wicked soul living actor do "revenge and break" then righteous soul living actor feel so hard, in this time righteous soul living actor not to be disappeared in the road to the righteous soul living in destination place, so that righteous soul living actor strongly living of righteous soul living behavior "it shared time with other, help other but also doing real love other"

Truly, there is no wicked soul, mind level living actor if righteous soul "me" living running to the righteous soul living, at that time all is shown to "thinking of wicked soul" "thinking of wicked soul" endless supplied wicked soul "thinking of wicked souls",

This "thinking of wicked soul" do effect in the "wicked soul me and mind level me", therefore if living in wicked soul then "wicked soul & thinking" is naturally follows of living, all of living decision from "thinking of wicked soul" then, direct to the wicked soul living in destination place.

Wicked soul thinking is produce fear, peace broken, so many same time and space living actors all damaged cause of following "thinking of wicked soul".

Righteous soul living behavior is "it time with other, help other but also doing real love other" in this case, in the natural of mind level living actor center for me, but righteous soul living actor "there is no thinking of wicked soul so that there is no me" righteous soul living is not me but other. Because there is no me, truly righteous soul living actor "there is no me", this is real living.

If do real living then, there is no to be target from wicked soul living actor "revenge and break", so then righteous soul me living in excitement, righteous soul living actor me excitement is prime concerning to real living me.

In the real living world, righteous soul "ME" living in excitement is better to me, but my living is not excitement, because what I'm doing all is not living in righteous soul living, I'm living in righteous soul living world but truly around of me all are shape of wicked soul living.

Even all of TV program most wicked soul living contents so my living is so simple, until then I'm not perfect living in righteous soul living, but I believe that my righteous soul living in real living.

Voyage 16days

Wicked soul living is cloudy in the righteous soul living place. Wicked soul living also living in the macro concept world, wicked soul living is doing not know living righteous soul living existence.

So that wicked soul living of ignorance of righteous soul living, under the wicked soul living an actor of macro concept world.

This wicked soul living actor keep living in "easy living" do not know hard living of righteous soul living actor "it shared time with other, help other, and doing real love other"

In the wicked soul of cloudy day, then it also living is true, righteous soul living is fine clear sky living. This is macro concept world explain, but truly micro concept world, is fine and clear is righteous soul, so called do not changed eternity time and space.

But cloudy is move to a place, or disappeared in the righteous soul living world time and space, so that cloudy is changed and disappeared from righteous soul living world.

This is compare of eternity blank space, just there is no writing alphabets, writing is changed but blank space is eternity same, this is truth.

In the micro concept world, righteous soul is blank space, wicked soul is alphabets.

Wicked soul living is cloudy in the righteous soul living world, so that micro concept world, righteous soul living actor see only wicked soul living of cloudy.

In the micro concept world, wicked soul of cloudy is changing of rainy, windy, snowy, storm, typhoon, if I be wicked soul living then I will be in the living of cloudy is changing of rainy, windy, snowy, storm, typhoon, but if living in the righteous soul living, then my living is blank space of just see wicked soul living move, change thing.

This is micro concept world, so that it never changed righteous soul living actor and changed wicked soul living actor, so that in the micro concept world, just watcher is righteous soul living actor, but seen to the righteous soul living, then they are all changed things so that there all wicked souls.

If watching righteous soul keep waken then still all of situations, righteous soul living is doing not swept away from wicked soul of rainy, windy, snowy, storm, typhoon, but if sleep righteous soul, then righteous soul "me" is swept away from wicked soul, so then there is no righteous soul "me", it already righteous soul "me" is damaged from wicked soul rainy, windy, snowy, storm, typhoon.

Wicked soul living is cloudy; cloud is also living, but cloudy is keep changing from cloudy to rainy, snow, windy all, but this is macro concept world 'me' is so hard living.

Macro concept world "me" is being wicked soul living, because micro concept world, righteous soul living actor is swept away from wicked soul, so macro concept world me is "there is no righteous soul" so long, macro concept "me" is in the wicked soul living actor of damaged from wicked soul so that all of living of dangerous living.

Please living excitement free from wicked soul living. I want to live in the righteous soul living in excitement. I do not want to be living in wicked soul excitement.

Wicked soul living excitement is "easy living" so long, drinking alcoholic beverage, but also sex, game, gambling etc.

But righteous soul living in excitement is "poor & hard living of" "it shared time with other, help other but also doing real love other" this is righteous soul living actor excitement.

Truly righteous soul "ME" living macro concept world, wicked soul living actor, mind level living actors, but rare of wicked soul living actors are mixed living now living. So that Righteous soul "ME" hard to live in excitement.

"Wicked soul living is cloudy" this living world also same living actor of "wicked soul +mind+ body" living, so then, wicked soul living actor rule is governing, so that in this place, nothing appeared of righteous soul living actor behavior " it shared time with other, help other, but also doing real love other", but wicked soul living world living actor "easy living" using "revenge and break other" so that in this place is so critical.

Truly wicked soul living world, if someone saying ' it shared time with other, help other, but also doing real love other" then righteous soul me is very shame because, righteous soul living behavior is become old.

Righteous soul living behavior "it shared time with other, help other, but also doing real love other" is so old, in the wicked soul living world, righteous soul living forgotten already.

Righteous soul "me" hard to live just morning "greeting of good morning" then all of living actor see me strange, "he must be mad", in the elevator righteous soul "me" "hi" then I felt so "embarrassing" it is, so that righteous soul "me" is so feel alone.

Righteous soul "ME" living in the wicked soul living world of changeable of cloudy living, so that living is not true but changeable living knowledge there is not used do not changed eternity living real living true knowledge, so righteous soul living me is seeking righteous soul living in excitement.

Voyage 17days

Righteous soul living is running to the Righteous soul living in destination is the same as dynamic arising sun in the morning to fall to under the ground sunset of beautiful and the same as trees spring season green color leaf and run to colorful leaf.

On the way workplace, by the way tree of color are so beautiful leaves. Beautiful leaves must be run for now beautiful leaves which make excitement macro concept world actors.

Colorful leaves do workers all the day, even just day and night, day create oxygen, night create carbon dioxide endless did.

While leaves helped fruit to birth and grow and harvest matured living.

Colorful leaves are all hard living then reaches at the colorful leaves to give excitement to the macro concept world living actor; wicked soul living actor, righteous soul living actor, but also mind level living actor. it must be so excitement with colorful leaves by the real living of righteous soul living actor.

Righteous soul living actor, colorful leaves and sunset all governed righteous soul living in destination place living actor of creation of knowledge.

Infer that righteous soul living in destination place is righteous soul living actors, colorful leaves and sunset etc.

Righteous soul living in destination place, it is "it shared time with others, help others, but also doing real love others" righteous soul living in destination place living actors are all lived in the macro concept world.

Birth to the macro concept world "wicked soul + righteous soul + mind + body" after that "Righteous soul +(wicked soul +mind) + body" as getting mind is 1/, wicked soul and mind must be infer that disappeared from righteous soul living actor,

so then it created in the end "righteous soul +body" here is (Righteous soul +body) is as body is shelter of righteous soul living so that it be create of Righteous soul living actor in the macro concept world, this moment safe returning to the righteous soul living in destination place.

After returning then righteous soul living actor being "nothing" so that righteous soul living actor safe returning to the righteous soul living in destination place, safe returning righteous soul must be same as Sunset, colorful leaves which make excitement to macro concept living actors, the same as safe returning righteous soul can give so excitement to the righteous soul living in destination place righteous soul living actors with god.

"Birth to the macro concept world "wicked soul + righteous soul + mind + body" after that "Righteous soul + (wicked soul +mind) + body" as getting mind is 1/∞, wicked soul and mind must be infer that disappeared"

This is macro concept world righteous soul living actor. While mind level living actor and wicked soul living actor also living.

If righteous soul living actor lost the way of righteous soul living in destination place, then after that living in mind level living actor of "getting much more than others"

Then, it must be damaged variable of wicked soul living actor of "easy living" so that mind level living actor must be changed into easily wicked soul living actor, so then it must be create wicked soul appeared.

If lived wicked soul living, then it must be slaver of wicked soul living actor Satan do "revenge and break" so that wicked soul must be damaged by other wicked soul living actors.

Righteous soul living actor try to keep running for the righteous soul living in destination place with doing sharing with other, helping other but also doing real love other. This is safe living just like safe being beautiful Sunset, beautiful colorful leaves.

Voyage 18days

Wicked soul living actor acting tunnel is "thinking of wicked soul" so that Thinking is wicked soul, then macro concept world wicked soul, righteous soul, mind level living actor question how to discriminate righteous soul living actor of micro concept tunnel "-1/~+1/

Then here is wicked soul "thinking of wicked soul", righteous soul micro concept tunnel "-1/∞~+1/∞".

Wicked soul living actor keep produce problems, through "thinking of wicked soul" remind anger, or revenge memory, keep pushing into macro concept world living actor behavior of "revenge and break".

Righteous soul living actor must watching wicked soul living "thinking of wicked soul".

Righteous soul living actor keep watching out "thinking of wicked soul" then righteous soul living actor between micro concept world and macro concept world righteous soul living actor being safe.

Macro concept world living actor all has "righteous soul, wicked soul living" righteous soul living actor how to live is decide, macro concept world living actor is righteous soul or wicked soul living is decide.

Wicked soul living actor best living place is an ignorance living actor, anger living actor, deceit living actor, to get much money even all use, then wicked soul living actor endless give "thinking of wicked soul" then wicked soul living actor get accepting "thinking of wicked soul" then do macro concept world living actor do "revenge and break" so then, wicked soul living actor win to the not wicked soul living actor of righteous soul, and mind level living actor.

Wicked soul living actor what he/she wanted thing is done by follows of "thinking of wicked soul", then wicked soul living actor living "easy living" is accomplished, truly wicked soul "easy living" is without input required to be getting,

So that wicked soul living actor must be related with other wicked soul living actor anger, so that other wicked soul living actor also follows "thinking of wicked soul" so that other wicked soul do "revenge and break", this chain is keep so that win of the game, the wicked soul soon being failure.

Truly real living of macro concept world living actor most living actor easily do follow "thinking of wicked soul", because this living is easy, do not pay hard procedure, but also do not pay to get after living, so that, macro concept world living actor accept "thinking of wicked soul", these are stealth technology, deceit other money, run the cur road which is do not hard course, these all be followed from "thinking of wicked soul".

Wicked soul follows of "thinking of wicked soul" then; somehow it goes faster than righteous soul living actor doing something.

Righteous soul living actor follow the micro concept tunnel "-1/~+1/" righteous soul living actor, all of effort to do, all procedures are keep followed, so that all almost Righteous soul living actor so tired to get solving on the problems, so that still righteous soul living actor effort to get it, then in a moment open the tunnel of micro concept so that righteous soul meet micro concept world righteous soul living in destination place righteous soul who try to help macro concept world living righteous soul living actor.

Wicked soul living actor follows "thinking of wicked soul" is done of other sacrifice, but righteous soul living actor follows of "micro concept tunnel meeting righteous soul" this is never other do harmed then achieve righteous soul living actor have been wanted thing.

So that wicked soul living actor winning is short termed reach at failure but, righteous soul living actor solving the problems is being eternity keep safe going.

Furthermore this is creative knowledge so that this micro concept tunnel getting solving knowledge is keep used after generation, it must be wicked soul living actor also use because wicked soul living actor it never do creative knowledge because why creative knowledge is from righteous soul living in destination place.

Voyage 19days

Righteous soul "me" lost righteous soul living ways. truly really lost righteous soul "me", at now I do not know who am i?

It must be I'm front line, out of righteous soul living road but now righteous soul and wicked soul front line living.

This is very fit to this book name "wicked soul do "revenge and break" righteous soul living actor"

Then wicked soul me "revenge me and try to break me" at now wicked soul me is stronger than righteous soul me.

Last night dinner time, I eat with fellow workers, where I was heard from him, he said "he live excitement with playing woman friend"

"He said that 2 times meet woman friend, but also he try to gift woman friend birthday value of 500000 won, here is woman friend is out of family living, who now living in marriage living.

I was temptation from his story telling, I felt that I am collapsed, my dam was broken, truly I'm land down to the wicked soul major of mind level living place.

I was thought that this is also one way of living, physical strong time; playing woman friend is also living values, truly my 40 years era I was do followed same of the way of living.

But this all not real that was all deceit and falsehood living, woman friend is why out of her family, husband, who is living is right, it is not living of righteous soul living sure.

Somehow changed from this, on the way workplace, the I saw who so early morning, a woman carried a big dog, her living who question whose behavior is wrong, living animal is who criticize woman carriage dog.

But out of mind level living, then it must be clear of wicked soul living righteous soul living behavior is "it shared time with other, and help other, but also doing real love other"

Righteous soul living actor living with other, not animal, excitement living with other macro concept world living actor, for example who live with dog, then macro concept actor do not live behavior od righteous soul living, so that macro concept living actor do not have loving target of other macro concept actor.

Here is loving target is truly hard, because loving target who are now wicked soul, or righteous soul, so that macro concept of living with dog, choose do living is better than wicked soul macro concept living actor.

So that living with dog who do not live in righteous soul living, then who will be damaged from other is directly "me" just do not do live in righteous soul living.

Do not living in righteous soul living without loving target, so then it must be easy living, anger of wicked soul living, so long not to do, as righteous soul of " it shared time with other, help other, but also doing real love other"

Righteous soul living so hard living, all of mind level living place, is trying to living easy living.

Hard living, is solving problems, then this living learn the knowledge to solve problems, this also required, so that macro concept world living place, most living actor is "wicked soul and mind level living actor" these actors are " get much more than others, but also living easy living"

In this place, righteous soul living behavior "it shared time with other, and help other, but also doing real love other" is so hard, so then in macro concept world living place, women are all try to do living "easy living"

So that it happens women conflict with men, then it must be natural, righteous soul, then love each other is natural, this is hetero love living, but wicked soul living place, hetero gender also do not love each other.

So that wicked soul living actor "do not love other" so then how to live, keep consistence do not love hetero living. All of real living is hard and suffer living, so then, out of righteous soul living in to righteous soul living then; it must be living of hard, suffered living.

Righteous soul "me" run out of righteous soul living running road, this road running living is not easy living, so hard and suffering living,

Righteous soul living accept doing righteous soul living, this is real so that real living is suffering, hard living so that some of hard living going with wicked soul living, righteous soul living actor behavior "it shard time with other, help other, but also doing real love other"

Righteous soul living actor do not lost do real love target it is very real living, so that if me, and wife and son and daughter, but righteous soul "me" do real love my wife, son and daughter.

Righteous soul "ME" I will keep do real love my wife, my son, my daughter, but righteous soul "ME" keep do real love them it is righteous soul living behavior.

Righteous soul "ME" I will do real love forever eternity, righteous soul "ME" living is do real love others including wicked soul living actor, righteous soul living actor, but also do living mind living actor also.

Righteous soul "ME" doing real love, wicked soul "revenge and break" then, wicked soul does living strongly, but righteous soul living actor do not do diligently then, righteous soul living in destination place, depart to voyage all travelers are all miss, so righteous soul living "ME" living do real love other, is only save wicked soul to righteous soul living actor.

At least righteous soul living actor mission of macro concept world is "do love lover who is now wicked or righteous soul, but so strong do real love lover to make righteous soul living actor, then carry her to the place of righteous soul living in destination place.

Righteous soul living way is so hard'

Going with other living

Help other living

Do real love other living

This is righteous soul living.

The result of righteous soul living is secure of certainty reach at the righteous soul living in destination place.

Truly now righteous soul "ME" for a while, I said discard all wicked soul from righteous soul me, then this is not truth of knowledge, so then I will do real love my wife, and my son and daughter.

Righteous soul living behavior is just micro concept world living me, so then righteous soul me keep doing real love other, but also do help other, and shared time with other this is real living.

On today I will keep doing real love; righteous soul of my wife and son and daughter.

Righteous soul "ME" doing real love other, this is eternity living.

Eternity doing real love other is prime my living in this macro concept world.

Voyage 20days

Macro concept living actor

God of righteous soul

Evil of wicked soul

Just living in macro concept world is just one so that so value, how to live is very important, but time and space is so short.

A macro concept world living actor living direction must be variable, one is wicked soul living destination place, and the other is righteous soul living in destination place.

If one is run for the wicked soul living in destination place then the one must be being Evil, the other run for the righteous soul living in destination place then it must be being Righteous soul God.

In moment, just micro concept point (-1/~+1/) through micro concept tunnel I met righteous soul, so that how to live is real, then micro concept point, it appeared the one is run for God, the other run for Evil.

So long, even in the macro concept point, all of actor living place, wicked soul, righteous soul, mind level living actor. so that righteous soul living actor if run for the righteous soul living directions then wicked soul run for wicked soul, so that righteous soul living actor help other to go for the righteous soul living in destination place,

But wicked soul living actor to go for the wicked soul living in destination place, do revenge and break, to make disturbance of making ignorance so that do not know righteous living destination place existence.

But truly, macro concept world living actor must be result is these destination place, so that who knows living destination place, then it must be trying to live righteous soul living.

But truly, living in the macro concept world living actor, do not know their living way is all be real, but going ignorance, so that how to live is so important.

Righteous soul "ME" must be live real living with righteous soul living knowledge, so it clear of running to the righteous soul living in destination place.

Truly righteous soul "ME" living is running to the righteous soul living, then the direction light and broadcasting is helping real living then safe reach at the righteous soul living in destination place.

Righteous soul living actor must do righteous soul living behavior "it shared time with other, help other, and doing real love other"

So that wicked soul living direction macro concept world actor do not know where is righteous soul living destination place, so that by doing righteous soul living behavior of "it shared time with other, help other, and doing real love other"

Righteous soul living actor save from evil and wicked soul, to righteous soul living and god, this is so important to righteous soul living actor.

Please Righteous soul "ME" important role is to help do not know righteous soul living in destination place, Righteous soul "ME" keep saying do live in righteous soul living then you will go for righteous soul living in destination place. Just one time living righteous soul living is how important it is, mind=1/, righteous soul living is itself is excitement living.

Righteous soul "ME" living real living running to the righteous soul living in destination place, my living is so hard living, suffer living.

But I will go for righteous soul living in destination place. I will do write a book silently.

While I'm writing book then I'm going deeper going, so my living is keep running t the deeper place, the place are righteous soul living in destination place.

As keep writing book then, righteous soul "ME" creation of knowledge must be deep realizing.

This is righteous soul "ME" running to the God of righteous soul living place. Righteous soul me is living with God.

Voyage 20days

Micro concept is "-1/~+1/" is time and space. Here time is end and begin, but space is time governing space. Here is micro concept is time and space.

Time is recognized in the macro concept world, end closed but also open the begin, so that righteous soul living actor, every living is result and cause, here is micro concept is result is first, but cause is last, here is some of compare is result is harvest, but cause is sowing.

Micro concept place is time and space combined expression as concept of macro concept world. Truly macro concept world time and space is this.

Micro concept place has space of field, so that agricultural field, wild field, but also mountain etc. cause of micro concept is sowing in the micro concept place, then end of time, then harvest of sowing.

In the micro concept place, harvest and sowing is keep continued, in the micro concept point (-1/~+1/) is not discriminate in the macro concept world.

Macro concept world living world living actor all followed micro concept (-1/ ~+1/) end but begin, macro concept world living actor must be realized with end and begin, here is closed past end, then just run for the future and righteous soul living in destination place.

If macro concept world living actor; end and beginning compare of micro concept (-1/~+1/), if macro concept world living actor get end of result, but do not begin of cause then, micro concept (-1/~+1/) then macro concept world living actor do not follow micro concept point concept, all of micro concept is running to the righteous soul living in destination place.

Here is micro concept is "-1/~+1/" is result then cause, so then macro concept world living actor must be excitement after soon comes hard living, because beginning is leaning and all of be test to get on, just all of hard process getting. if macro concept world living actor do not follow micro concept then, if comes excitement then remained in the excitement time and space, then in the place do not running to the righteous soul living in destination place, in the end that place is changed into wicked soul living in destination place.

Righteous soul living actor keep follows of micro concept "-1/~+1/" so then macro concept world actor of living righteous soul living actor runs; end then right time begin, so that truly there is no easy living, but excitement is energy to begin to the new righteous soul living in destination place running, the beginning is so hard to be finish the project, so long all of energy is connect end but begin, if macro concept world living actor do not living end of excitement is right after beginning of hard living.

But if macro concept world living actor do not follow micro concept point living, then truly macro concept living actor out of righteous soul living actor.

Righteous soul living actor running cell is micro concept point"-1/~+1/, righteous soul living actor runs to the righteous soul living in destination place, so then micro concept point is all of righteous soul living actor running points.

Even micro concept world is point, but these are in the scene of macro concept point is not a point but the line, if a line is broken then the time is out of running to the righteous soul living in destination place.

Righteous soul living actor living actor must be keeping in line to the righteous soul living in destination place. Righteous soul living actor is not easy living, hard living but excitement keep procedure of reaching at the righteous soul living in destination place.

Micro concept "-1/" end and beginning, harvest and sowing, past and future, etc.

If macro concept place living actor run micro concept point, then the actor is living in righteous soul living, but if not the actor living is not living in righteous soul living.

Whoever else, in the macro concept world living actor try to live in easy living, then this is mind level living actor and wicked soul living actor, they do not know micro concept world living, cycle of macro concept world to micro concept world.

But if righteous soul living actor of turning between micro concept world and macro concept world, then this is real living, righteous soul so know that macro and micro is cycling.

This is same as seen of sun day time end then it start dim, dark of night, this is living, the same as if macro concept world living actor do thinking only living in day time then, night time what happened, but all of living actor living in day and night.

Righteous soul living actor in the micro concept world living is excitement, but wicked soul living in the micro concept world is not like living in righteous soul living actor living.

But righteous soul living in the macro concept world is not easy living, but wicked soul living actor try to live in easy in macro concept world.

Under the sun macro concept world hard living is better than micro concept world unseen world hard living of wicked soul living in destination place living.

But macro concept world living is time of change time, an macro concept world living actor all possible to live in righteous soul living, if macro concept world living actor hard under the unseen world wicked soul living in destination place, then all is not other, but all is "me", because all of living actor same opportunity to be changed in to righteous soul living.

But macro concept world living "easy living" then this is wicked soul living, but "hard living, hard problems living" is "it shared time with other, help other, but also doing real love other" then it is the hard living, because ignorance living actor behavior is so hard to live with me.

Macro concept world living place all of living actors are such as wicked soul, mind level living actor, but also righteous soul living actor, so then, wicked soul living actor living standard, wicked soul living in living standard, then the place righteous soul living actor of doing righteous soul living behavior "it shared time with other, help other, but also doing real love other" is so hard, difficult problems.

Because all of living standard is so strong, mind level living actor living standard is all of time changed into money, wicked soul living actor time all is to be "easy living", so that righteous soul living behavior is " it shared time with other, help other, but also doing real love other".

Righteous soul living behavior is looked as means, lowered, because righteous soul living is not related with getting money, so that money getting interesting actors are scornful to the righteous soul living behavior.

Even righteous soul living actor try to live righteous soul living in the macro concept world, then the living is hard so that, most righteous soul living is just personal living inside living is this,

But also righteous soul living is not seen but unseen living in righteous soul living in the corner of the macro concept world living place.

A righteous soul living actor is running to the righteous soul living in destination place doing living of righteous soul living behavior.

Voyage 21days

If an actor make me hard then I will be suffer from it, then make hard living actor is using to be easy living "revenge and break" energy, then it must be I'm wicked soul, mind level living, but also I'm righteous soul living.

Then here is if I be live in wicked soul then, making hard wicked soul energy using to break me,

Then in the wicked soul living wicked soul me is getting clean of my sins, mind level living me also be cleaned of my sins, but also righteous soul me also be cleaned even dusty of sins.

So that if an actor really make hard then it is rolling to me, a cleaner.

This is seen in the Buddha "book of diamond sutra".

Voyage 22days

What makes me now?

It must be cause and result; this is kept in me also. So then "thinking of wicked soul" seeding in a place, this seeding it will grows also, "thinking of wicked soul" to make harvest of "thinking of wicked soul do fruit of wicked soul behavior"

Yes cause and result, so that righteous soul living actor meet through micro concept point "-1/~+1/" meet righteous soul, between macro concept world righteous soul and micro concept world righteous soul, so that macro concept world righteous soul to be " it shared time with macro concept world righteous soul, help righteous soul, but also to be real loved from micro concept world righteous soul" so that macro concept world righteous soul get new fresh creation of knowledge to get macro concept world, so that righteous soul living actor cause is result is micro concept point"-1/~+1/" this is true living, so that this living actor of righteous soul living actor can go for the righteous soul living, so called righteous soul living actor runs to the righteous soul living in destination place.

At now me is "wicked soul living actor"

At now me is "righteous soul living actor"

At now me is "wicked soul living actor" then

"Thinking of wicked soul" is lead macro concept world wicked soul "ME" then, "me" feeling is anger, fear, revenge and break etc.

"Thinking of wicked soul" if keep thinking then it seed wicked soul living cause, so that wicked soul living actor safe living of wicked soul living, because in the place, already seeded growing of "thinking of wicked soul", this will be felt of macro concept world living "ME" is all is the wicked soul behavior all is turn to me, so that all of cause of thinking of wicked soul in the do damaged to me.

At now me is "righteous soul living actor" then

"Hearing broadcasting from righteous soul living in destination place" this is all of information how to run, solve problems all of running to the righteous soul living in destination place.

Truly reading book then all of living enlighten, so their living of righteous soul living creation of knowledge is same, then, it must be broadcasting contents are all same, because righteous soul living actor running road is all to be righteous soul living in destination place.

At now me is "wicked soul living actor"

At now me is "righteous soul living actor"

At now mw is "wicked soul living actor" then macro concept "ME" is stop to running righteous soul living in destination place.

Stop running righteous soul living in destination place, so that, wicked soul living actor living in the past.

At now me is "righteous soul living actor" then macro concept "ME" is keep running to the righteous soul living in destination place

Keep running righteous soul living actor running to the righteous soul living in destination place, so that righteous soul actor living is in the future living.

Do not run to the future then do live in closed out of past, so that wicked souls are living make hard other living, because stop running, so that past knowledge is better, all of wicked soul living actor past knowledge is living criteria

But righteous soul living actor is keep changed all of knowledge, micro concept point is move to the future, so that any time and place is not same situation, so that all of righteous soul living actor, keep fresh and clear of new creation of knowledge getting.

Righteous soul living actor do not make hard each other, because new knowledge is solve the problems so that righteous soul living behavior is " it shared time with other, and help other, but also doing real love other".

Then the living is so excitement living. But also help each other; do real love each other, this is living in righteous soul living.

Voyage 23days

"Thinking of wicked soul" keeps watching and disturbance hearing broadcasting from righteous soul living in destination place.

Truly in the feeling of macro concept world living "Thinking of wicked soul" and "broadcasting from wicked soul" is not discriminate.

In the feeling of macro concept world living actor "thinking of wicked soul" is all, so that wicked soul living actor follow of "thinking of wicked soul" so that wicked soul living actor follow the "thinking of wicked soul"

But righteous soul living actor follows " broadcasting from righteous soul" so then, righteous soul living actor do live with hearing broadcasting but wicked soul do live with "thinking of wicked soul".

This is to understand of macro concept world then, if sleep righteous soul living then, wicked soul fully follows " thinking of wicked soul" then during this time, righteous soul living actor disappeared from macro concept world living.

This means that righteous soul living running hearing broadcasting from righteous soul living in destination place.

Why righteous soul "ME" is awaken is this, Righteous soul "ME" living mission is do real love lover, make lover righteous soul then live in excitement, but if lover is now still living wicked soul living then, help to be righteous soul, but also only power effect of doing real love lover then, the lover is being righteous soul living.

But also, lover condition is strong wicked soul then, it must be righteous soul me, if do not awaken me, then lover of wicked soul also effect to me, so that righteous soul me be changed in to wicked soul also, so that wicked soul is make hard to running to the righteous soul living in destination place.

Wicked soul is make hard righteous soul living actor running to the righteous soul living, this is righteous soul living actor wicked soul of lover to make righteous soul, this is righteous soul living actor voyage purpose, meet lover help lover to be live in righteous soul living then, running with lover to the righteous soul living in destination place.

Righteous soul living actor living only using tool is "do real love other" living with wicked soul living.

Strangely, wicked soul use energy of "revenge and break" so long, wicked soul of lover power is "revenge and break" so that righteous soul living is so hard with wicked soul living of lover.

Righteous soul living actor do carry do real loving " lover" then make change lover to be righteous soul, but also righteous soul living actor running to the righteous soul living in destination place, to do that hearing broadcasting from righteous soul living in destination place.

Wicked soul living actor all located a righteous soul living actor place, it never helping righteous soul living running for the righteous soul living in destination place.

Righteous soul living around truly, living wicked soul, some of living role of making hard righteous soul, but also other are the army of wicked soul to make disappeared from now, so that, righteous soul living actor is target to the wicked soul "revenge and break" if this strong wicked soul attack righteous soul living actor then it must be disappeared from now.

So long, righteous soul living actor makes hide not be seen from wicked soul, it must be distance from wicked soul living place which is living "easy living".

As that righteous soul living is "hard living" so that righteous soul living is not same of easy living, so that hard living is "the poor & righteous soul living" is only living in the macro concept world.

But also righteous soul living actor as approach to the righteous soul living in destination place, then righteous soul living actor being "righteous soul & nothing" so in this time wicked soul do not see, "righteous soul & nothing" then, it must be righteous soul living actor being safe living, which is not do harmed from wicked soul living actor.

If righteous soul me, then approach to the righteous soul living in destination place, righteous soul "me" is righteous soul & nothing, but also, in this time string righteous soul is righteous soul mission make change lover to righteous soul, living righteous soul lover and me is living in excitement as mission clear of righteous soul living.

So then righteous soul & nothing, is not seen to the wicked soul living actor, so that living in righteous soul living, it accomplished safe living of righteous soul living actor.

In this time, macro concept me is so peace living, because there is no "thinking of wicked soul" to me.

In righteous soul me perfect "thinking of wicked soul=1/ " so then macro concept world living actor living in righteous soul living.

Righteous soul living me is righteous soul= so then in this time righteous soul living actor feeling is so peace, so excitement living.

But also can hear broadcasting from righteous soul living in destination place without any disturbance of "thinking of wicked soul" living in macro concept world, with shelter of body, but righteous soul living same place of as body is disappeared from righteous soul living me, as safe reach body disappeared then, righteous soul safe returning to the righteous soul living in destination place.

Wicked soul is just make hard righteous soul, in the end a righteous soul living actor disappeared from running to the righteous soul living in destination place.

Truly only righteous soul is living in macro concept world, but make hard to run righteous soul living in destination place, disturbance role is wicked soul, so that wicked soul is just tool, not a purpose, so that if a living actor in the macro concept world living, as wicked soul living, then the living actor is not related with righteous soul living, so that wicked soul is segregated from righteous soul living.

In the micro concept world, truly righteous soul is eternity living, but wicked soul is changed living actor so that all of wicked soul is occur and disappeared.

Wicked soul living actor role is only disturbing righteous soul living actor running to the righteous soul living in destination place.

How to live be real living is clear, righteous soul living is real living. Wicked soul living is "easy living" if macro concept world living is easy living then, an actor living is never safe returning to the righteous soul living.

So that righteous soul living actor " it shared time with other, help other, and do real love other" this is not easy living, but this living is not compared with wicked soul, mind level living, so that righteous soul living actor keep running to the righteous soul living in destination place.

Voyage 24days

Why righteous soul "me" is influenced from other manners?

Righteous soul "me" living in macro concept with wicked soul living actor, mind level living actor.

Here is righteous soul living actor behavior is "it shard time with other, help other, but also doing real love other"

Wicked soul living actor behavior is "easy living" and to be easy living using "revenge and break other"

Mind level living actor behavior is "getting much more than others"

Righteous soul "Me" meet wicked soul living actor behavior, but also mind level living actor behavior, then it must be influence me so that, righteous soul "ME" connect energy righteous soul me and wicked soul others, in a moment, occupied all me by the wicked soul living actor energy.

In this case, righteous soul "me" how to get over the situation, in me sea is occur rainstorms so that in me all is influenced that the peace in me is broken. cause of it occur anger, so that righteous soul "me" is what I said then broken peace, now is not peace, this time so important because of righteous soul "me" must be survived from this situations.

Because this rainstorm will be disappeared from righteous soul "ME", it clear peace will comes then; overcoming righteous soul "me" must be growing.

Righteous soul living "ME" keep influenced from out or in, because out is living with wicked soul living actor and mind level living actors, in is very important, this is so variable but this lead me do it, so that I'm fear on that, in living micro concept world d wicked soul do in play to do, last night, I was earlier resting from job, so that I rarely early sleeping tried, then in me, aroused temptation, but also why do wicked soul behavior come to me; pm 7 I try to sleep, then I do not sleep early, try to do sleep, then in a moment wicked soul living actor all occupied, so that I carried wicked soul living actor do behavior, so that even I do not wanted to be wicked soul, but I be in wicked soul living, so that I did wicked soul living behavior is "easy living in excitement" so that, I lost righteous soul living " it shared time with other, help other, but also doing real love other of excitement" hard to live righteous soul living.

Doing living righteous soul living "out of wicked soul, mind level living actor behavior influence" and "in of wicked soul living actor behavior of influence" ultimate, righteous soul living actor be awaken to watch wicked soul living "revenge and break" then righteous soul living is keep running to the righteous soul living in destination place.

Running to the righteous soul living in destination place is macro concept world living "ME" feeling is "peace", this is real living.

Wicked soul living actor behavior; the living actor also do work every times, but also wicked soul see wicked soul, and other living also, wicked soul living actor can see discriminate clear who is enemy or not, so that, wicked soul living actor is so well to live in macro concept living.

But actually it is not clear who is wicked soul, who is not, but this is happened in the manners, so that, good manners are must be living fully "it shared time with other, help other, but also doing real love other", good manners are so closed living of righteous soul living, but bad manners are possible to be living in wicked soul living.

If some special do bad manners righteous soul "ME" then righteous soul "ME" recognition is false, but truly not, bad manners living actor must be possible in wicked soul living is.

Righteous soul "me" living is tried to run to the righteous soul living in destination place. Because righteous soul living actor world is macro and micro all of concept world is open so that, seen and unseen world living is keep continued. all of living is seen and unseen, macro and micro all living is comes to me, sometime will come to me, micro concept world living, unseen world living, but also the other will be living in the macro concept world living, seen world living but also, the actor also soon reach at the micro concept world living destination place of righteous soul, or wicked soul living in place.

How to know this truth, but mind level living actor do not know, so that living in the macro concept world seen world living is only living, so there is no fear of which locate micro concept world unseen world, so here righteous soul me called mind level living actor as ignorance living actor.

Truly experienced hard living in the unseen world of micro concept world living actor, lived in try to easy living, but also do revenge and break living, so that, wicked soul living actor living, do live that

This is piety to the righteous soul living actor, so that righteous soul living actor comes to save lover from who live in wicked soul, so that righteous soul living actor know that righteous soul living in destination place living was so excitement, the righteous soul living actor try to save lover bring back to the righteous soul living in destination place.

Righteous soul living actor mission in the macro concept world, is do make lover righteous soul living actor then living lover, comeback safe to the righteous soul living in destination place.

Wicked soul and righteous soul is soul to the mind level living actors, but mind level living actor is ok to get use the soul energy to get much more than others, so long, mind level living actor, if do can use wicked soul living energy then "easy living" so that keep use wicked soul living energy, then being wicked soul living is natural living.

Most ignorance living actor being to wicked soul living in the macro concept world living. macro concept world living place are all occupied by the wicked soul then, truly, wicked soul living actor all use "revenge and break" so that macro concept world living place, all of living actor to get "easy living" then all wicked soul living place, to try to get much more big game is occurred.

Macro concept world wicked soul living actor, to get big so that wicked soul power is combined to big one to get big energy, to be "easy living" then, truly, big wicked soul, actor, or small power of actors are all be target of a big wicked soul living actor so that, the big wicked soul living actor do "revenge and break others" this is big broken the place just like in the macro concept world seen world comes to the disaster or much more than huge disaster war.

If righteous soul runs to the righteous soul living in destination place just one of all, then the place is righteous soul living energy is influence so that the place is not be critical broken, because righteous soul living actor one must be safe returning to the righteous soul living in destination place.

If righteous soul living actor just one, is disappeared from the place, then the place it occur by among pure all of wicked soul living actor "revenge and break others" so that in the place all be revenged from others, but also all to be broken by the other wicked soul living actors.

What is real living?

All of living actor has "righteous soul, wicked soul" so then which living is all selected by actor itself, if an actor do live in righteous soul living then the actor living must be living against to the wicked soul living, so that all of easy living of wicked soul enemy.

But all of hard living but living righteous soul living then, if an righteous soul living actor defense to broken war.

To be live righteous soul living is getting peace only.

Voyage 25days

Wicked soul living actor do "revenge and break" still not be in "nothing" but still live in "something of righteous soul living actor".

Living in this macro concept world, if living do nothing, but still righteous soul "me" is not feel safe but also not peace, why, macro concept world righteous soul "ME" needed to be recognized to be, this is just "wicked soul living actor do "revenge and break" seen and something all of souls, even wicked soul, so that "something righteous soul" must be target from wicked soul.

This is feeling in the macro concept world righteous soul strange, just something righteous soul, it still being target from wicked soul, so that still righteous soul "ME" possible to be disappeared from macro concept world. so that righteous soul do not survive then, being disappeared from running to the righteous soul living in destination place.

So long, righteous soul must be living from something to nothing in righteous soul living. Being "nothing" is being unseen righteous soul living, and then there is not seen to the wicked soul, so that being "righteous soul & nothing", this is perfect safe from wicked soul attacking.

Voyage 26days

Wicked soul living mission is "to be easy living, using revenge and break other".

If a living macro concept world, a living actor in wicked soul, then the actor must be role of "order does revenge other" and "as followed other revenge and break doing for other revenge affairs.

In this macro concept world living, then understand is all body, but here is wicked soul is not with body, but also righteous soul living also, so that, wicked soul living is feeling in the "thinking of wicked soul"

Wicked soul is transfer to wicked soul, so that, wicked soul information is traversed without keeping rule. wicked soul appeared any time and any place, so that if a living as wicked soul living then, the actor keep receiving wicked soul living information, but also "thinking of wicked soul" so that wicked soul mission is "revenge and break" so that in the point of wicked soul living that is usual, so that wicked soul do "revenge and break" is not a crime or sins.

If a wicked soul living occupied living place, then a wicked soul living actor to do "easy living" using "revenge and break" then it is all wicked soul living that way.

So that in a place, wicked soul living behavior is acted then, truly a righteous soul is almost to be disappeared from macro concept world.

Wicked soul living actor do not know righteous soul living behavior "it shared time with other, help other, but also doing real love other"

Novel Wicked Soul Do "Revenge and Break"

Wicked soul living actor common sense is to easy live using revenge and breaks other.

Righteous soul "ME" recently experiment on "wicked soul living actor doing case"

What I have been try to make righteous soul living, that is what I'm doing living with wife, so that I feel that my wife is what I to do, righteous soul living mission, so that I'm doing for her "it shared time with wife, and help wife, but also doing real love wife" then wife work place team working, then a team worker

Righteous soul "ME" recognition this case, wife is living in righteous soul living? "it shared time with other, help other, but also doing real love other"

If a person also righteous soul living behavior " it shared time with other, help other, but also doing real love other" so that person also keep anger to another, so then, both wicked soul living actor must be their living is usual, because of they are living as wicked soul living.

If a person keeps discriminate to another person from normal living, then the other person living is big anger, it is conflict between them, so then it is same living.

That person also but much more hard because f accusation, how it is important of "cosmos law" this is wicked soul living behavior then same replied as the method of wicked soul living behavior, so then, wicked soul living getting hard cause of wicked soul living.

Here is new, he must be learn because of doing not know, working history, experiment, but the young worker need to be learning, but a accuser just only "law fit or not is important" so that young living actor, must be learning, but also learning around but the new living of worker, straight against to the manager, then manager have working for so long, about same working, then this work is done, but worker said " this is not fit to the law", then in the end, this is must be if now living is majority is wicked soul then, it must be right to the accuser because " the law is fit", but in the righteous soul living point of view then " it shared time with other, help other, but also doing real love other" then, it must be young worker needed time to learning, so then, fully the team manager understand his wrong behavior

The accuser must be live in the 40 years living in a place, then it required to be learn the living method, but infer of wicked soul to live "easy living" the accuser living actor do not going deeper to other ways, of righteous soul living behavior so that, the accuser must be being hard to live longer in the work place.

How to live in this wicked soul living, so then in the real living if macro concept world living, an actor living is righteous soul living then how hard live is this case is learning.

It is so surprise in the official working job, in the team working, then team member did accuse, but also manager of infer wicked soul living actor, do not live righteous soul living behavior " it shared time with accuser, and help accuser, but also do real love accuser".

The living is not simple,

A person's sinful living is so deep so that, cosmos law requires to pay the sins, so that living cosmos law result is this, being hard because of her sinful living, here is not accuser bad behavior but, the accuser is role of wicked soul "revenge and break" so then, cosmos law, a god seek player of wicked soul living behaver so then, it must be her working place did,

It must be infer that, cosmos law, required me to make damage her, but infer of righteous soul "ME" is keep doing living in righteous soul living "it shared time with other, help other, but also doing real love other" so that righteous soul "ME" do not used wicked soul living actor, so that wicked soul living actor do "revenge and break" other revenge living actor.

If a living actor living in a wicked soul living actor, then sure of wicked soul living actor to be "revenge and break" this is general wicked soul living actor behavior.

Not to be "revenge and break other" then it must living out of wicked soul living, this is living of righteous soul living then, this living is being "righteous soul & nothing" it must be free from wicked soul living behavior of "revenge and break".

Not anymore living in wicked soul, then righteous soul living actor must be keep living righteous soul living, so that righteous soul will do living usual living is " it shared time with other, help other, but also doing real love other" so that all is doing solve itself.

All is righteous soul of righteous soul living in destination place, this is real living, and this is righteous soul living blessed from righteous soul living in destination place.

In the macro concept world, all of time is end of beginning so that end is easy living, but beginning is challenge a new stages, so that righteous soul living keep running to the righteous soul living in destination place, so that righteous soul is "beginning", but wicked soul living is "end living of easy living", so that in a moment all of living is managed righteous soul or wicked soul is resulting is a big difference, righteous soul living actor is do humble because a new living, but wicked soul "easy living" is wicked soul living is destination place so long anger to other, "easy living" breaking.

Voyage 27days

Wicked soul living actor to wicked soul living actor, how to do? Wicked soul living community is general "easy living" does revenge other and break other.

Wicked soul living community a wicked soul living actor common sense is "doing revenge other and break other", so that wicked soul living actor feeling is that is real, in the wicked soul living community, a righteous soul living actor living who is real living is "it shard time with other, help other, but also doing real love other"

Then, wicked soul living actor how feeling to a righteous soul living feeling and behavior, it must be infer that wicked soul living actor think that "that is so strange and foolish living actor".

Wicked soul living in community best prime thing is "easy living", here is "easy living is health, eat well, sleep well only wicked soul self", so that wicked soul living actor keep try to live in "easy living".

Wicked soul living actor try to easy living, then good wicked soul try to transient to righteous soul living being, the actor until then learn a new living of righteous soul, but wicked soul living actor even do good, but that is not righteous soul living, still living in wicked soul living, so that wicked soul living actor do live well is still has "revenge and break other".

It means that wicked soul try to righteous soul behavior is impossible, so that a living actor in the macro concept world, then wicked soul living actor behavior is seen point of righteous soul, then there is no righteous soul, but in the wicked soul run to the righteous soul living direction, then the wicked soul living actor still in the wicked soul living actor, so that wicked soul to wicked soul conflict, wicked soul to be living in righteous soul living then how to hard, so then wicked soul living is "easy living" to be living in righteous soul living is "hard living".

Wicked soul toward to the righteous soul living, then wicked soul keep living hard living, if an wicked soul did "revenge me and break me" even though, toward to run righteous soul living of wicked soul so hard not to do "revenge and break other". While hard cause of doing is not revenge and break is so hard, but endure of it, then just accumulate righteous soul living energy so then, in the end wicked soul living actor still have been running to the righteous soul living direction.

Infer that my lover is wicked soul living actor, but also lover work place a team member did accusation of wrong doer of doing actually lover did well in the law, so then an accusation team member false accusation, so wicked soul lover try to do "revenge and breaking a false accusation team member"

If lover running to the righteous soul living actor place, then an wicked soul of lover so hard not to do "revenge and break other", this is contrary to wicked soul behavior do righteous soul living so hard, but lover of wicked soul do not "revenge and break accusation wicked soul" then lover will be running to the righteous soul living place.

Wicked soul living lover lives in a wicked soul living community, but infer of righteous soul "me" is living in righteous soul living in "Me", because wicked soul community is general, but righteous soul living is not, just living in me only "righteous soul living place", so long, righteous soul "ME" toward lover of wicked soul, is so miss.

Wicked soul "lover" still lived, just toward wicked behavior but lover, try to be living in righteous soul living, but originality is wicked soul lover, so that lover can't love lover, because infer of wicked soul lover, so that righteous soul "me" is feeling is still reach me lover loving me, so then wicked soul living "lover" must be endure of doing not "revenge and break other". righteous soul "me" how to do wicked soul "love", righteous soul living actor do behavior "it shared time with other, help other, but also doing real love other", so then righteous soul "ME" do keep real love wicked soul "lover" that is only righteous soul "ME" doing.

Wicked soul "lover" try to be being righteous soul living, but lover is now living in wicked soul, so wicked soul lover is to live righteous soul living is not lover positon, so that living in righteous soul living is so high to the wicked soul "lover".

Righteous soul is higher to the wicked soul living actor, so that righteous soul living actor does living real lover the wicked soul "lover".

Living wicked soul, living righteous soul,

Living wicked soul is keep living in turbulence of problem maker,

Living righteous soul is keeping living is solving wicked soul problems.

Wicked soul living actor try to do live well, but result of living is wicked soul living, all of to be only living easy of wicked soul, so that create problems to other wicked soul, other righteous soul living.

Righteous soul living actor, undertake all problems of wicked soul, because righteous soul living behavior is "it shared time with other, help other, but also doing real love other".

Righteous soul "ME" lover of wicked soul, how to live, this is wicked soul living is "easy living" and "revenge and break other" so that wicked soul "lover" is fighter in lover living community, so that wicked soul living "lover" around all be not feeling like righteous soul behavior.

So then, how serious in macro concept world living, righteous soul living, and wicked soul living is important, wicked soul living is lower living to the righteous soul living who is living in high.

Wicked soul lower living is animal living, but righteous soul living is near to the god living. righteous soul living is end is righteous soul living in destination place, but wicked soul living actor end of macro concept world living then it reach at the wicked soul living in destination place.

Righteous soul living "ME" living actor must save wicked soul "lover" because wicked soul living is do not feel in real living of excitement.

Righteous soul "ME" really expect "wicked soul lover" being righteous soul living.

Righteous soul living "ME" "it shared with my lover, and do help lover but also I will do real love lover" then my wicked soul lover being changed into righteous soul of lover.

It required to righteous soul "ME" keep doing real love lover to make righteous soul living, then it must be mission clear righteous soul "ME" in the macro concept world living.

Righteous soul "ME" live righteous soul "lover" same reach at the righteous soul living in destination place, in the end, righteous soul "ME" righteous soul "lover" all is each other living in righteous soul living.

Voyage 28days

If wicked soul does "revenge and break" righteous soul living me then, it must be righteous soul living king of god, has a planning, as the righteous soul soldier, righteous soul "ME" must be "revenged and break" for the purpose of righteous soul sake.

At now, righteous soul "me" is urgent, because I want to land to live after 60 years.

Righteous soul "ME" try to buy as "real estate auction".

What happen to me, this is really possible "wicked soul do revenge and break righteous soul living "me".

If this buying is under the righteous soul, then righteous soul king, god permit me is prime concerning.

If my righteous soul "me" is still "the poor & righteous soul" then it possible by accident revenges my buy estate.

But if my living is wicked soul or righteous soul then, it must be all of power "revenge and break" is effect, so that my buying land will be blocked from wicked soul living actors.

But righteous soul "ME" clear of pure righteous soul living, then real of righteous soul living actors is being helped of wicked soul living actors' revenge and break righteous soul "ME".

Here is if my living is not righteous soul of mind level living, then it must be attacked from wicked soul of easy living actors.

Truly will I being living in righteous soul so that, righteous soul defense from wicked soul, then it must be come to me, what I wanted real estate will be being in as god gift, because righteous soul fight not to be revenge and broken from wicked souls.

Righteous soul "ME" try to share of what I'm real living behavior, as I'm approaching to the closing my first job, only 5 years remained so that, I have to prepared to live after retired my first job, so that I'm planning to buy real estate of mountain.

So I'm very urgent and all of mind is being increased, so that righteous soul living is being occupied by mind, so that righteous soul "me" is dangerous.

Truly much more important is " righteous soul's living", so that I expect righteous soul living king permit me, then righteous soul me is being clear, because god will give me gift by all of wicked soul living power all make less strong to my buying land.

All being possible buying is only done by righteous soul god permit me to get real estate. This is only safe without anything dangerous of wicked soul attacking to righteous soul "me".

If I got a possible what I want to get land is all is effort to get, the way of righteous soul living behavior; "it shared time with others, help others, but also doing real love other".

My lover is keep care of me whether being failure of invest, so that this buying estate would be, also, wicked soul can used "revenge and break" so that if living is wicked soul, then wicked soul do "revenge and break" other, so that revenge and break of being is, but other is me, so that to accomplish what try to do, is all of relating on buying "real of estate" then all be living in righteous soul is possible to depend of wicked soul's "revenge and break".

Will I be living in righteous soul living, this is so urgent, I'm fear of lover accept my planning to buy mountain to live after 60 years old.

If truly living "me" isliving in wicked soul, if they have enough money for buying what they want to get, as righteous soul "me" do not agreeable, because at that time, the me of wicked soul sure of attacking to other wicked soul, so that as wicked soul living getting really wanted thing is not permitted to get.

Righteous soul "ME" by accidently come to buy mountain, until then I did abandonment to buy mountain, but suddenly appeared to me to get mountain, so what shall I do, as righteous soul still do not know what happen to me.

This is really urgent to me, because I felt so hard to run to the future; if runs to the righteous soul living in destination place.

Until now, righteous soul "ME" so hard, because there is no excitement to me, living every day is so hard, then this is comes to me, as living of righteous soul is begin by mind=1/, so that true living of righteous soul "me".

If righteous soul strong power to defense me from wicked soul offence, then it must be I will get real estate, this is strong base to go for the righteous soul living in destination place.

Please god help me righteous soul "ME" getting real estate.

This means that righteous soul "ME" is helped, blessed to get it, righteous soul "me" living is righteous soul god will do gift, which can get mountain.

If there is not mind, then there is righteous soul living, then righteous soul living actor keep lived to increased righteous soul living energy, this is macro concept world, blessing, as open getting it, then god use my energy, giving to blessing.

This is not a problem of technique of biding but this is how to live is much more primed concerning thing to get a mountain.

If righteous soul "ME" is helped all of righteous soul then, it must be righteous soul living god, will permit me to get it.

If god permit me getting land then I will be living excitement because of tree seed germinate is very excitement to me.

Please righteous soul king, god please consider deeply, righteous soul "Me" is urgent, if urgent then help me, if not other righteous soul living actor use righteous soul energy, then I will be wait to come of auction bidding.

Please righteous soul king god permit me, open me for living of righteous soul living buying real estate, of mountain.

Voyage 29days

Righteous soul living "me" is living. If wicked soul living "ME" also go with me, wicked soul keep try to do mission of "revenge and break other".

If in the macro concept place living "me" is theory is 100% righteous soul living, wicked soul living, so then in the righteous soul is perfectly living of righteous soul, wicked soul.

Practically it is real living is mixed righteous soul, wicked soul, so that, so long macro concept world righteous soul and wicked soul is living.

It must be infer that righteous soul is feeling is Buddha scripture of "real me", wicked soul is "thinking of wicked soul" truly experimental then, wicked soul is ignorance.

Wicked soul living "ME" is basic of "revenge and break of easy living" wicked soul all of tools of revenge and break so only "me" easy living of only for me, there all be destroyed but only living me.

This is the point of view of righteous soul living

Then righteous soul feeling is so huge surprise, righteous soul of real me is all forgive so that forget and getting peace, then abruptly push in to righteous soul to do "revenge and break other" keep push into righteous soul living place, so that righteous soul do not want to see, but keep trying to show righteous soul "ME".

If righteous soul follow the wicked soul making anger making revenge other, then, it disappeared righteous soul, but appeared wicked soul in the place of righteous soul living actor seeing place.

Then wicked soul living is occupied in me, then macro concept actor feeling is gloomy and anger but also feel alone, all of metallic sickness out of order is coming.

If righteous soul living actor feel excitement is there is no seen to the righteous soul, just nothing then the righteous soul feel excitement.

Wicked soul living actor is live in, then wicked soul living of ignorance of righteous soul living of "it shared time with other, but also doing help other, and doing real love other".

As wicked soul of ignorance but doing "revenge and break other" here is other is wicked soul other is " include righteous soul me and other" so long, it is real living.

If wicked soul of ignorance living occupied in me, then macro concept world living actor do living wicked soul living behavior in the seen world "revenge and break" using this mission living of "easy living".

Wicked soul living "revenge and break" righteous soul "me" first target to be "revenge and break" so that, righteous soul "ME" first feeling gloomy, attacking righteous soul "ME", truly righteous soul "ME" is not other, but wicked soul me is make breaking righteous soul "ME".

Wicked soul living "ME" is against to the righteous soul "ME", truly there is no, do not know, the wicked soul, but righteous soul is real living, but righteous soul living do mission clear of " real love lover to make righteous soul" then it is wicked soul living actor making change lover from wicked soul to righteous soul living.

It means that righteous soul living actor do " it shared time lover of wicked soul, do help lover of wicked soul, but also do real love lover of wicked soul" so that wicked soul of lover being changed into righteous soul living.

While this wicked soul to be righteous soul living, then other wicked soul includes in me wicked soul also, keep "revenge and break it". Because of wicked soul is ignorance, just like animal living.

Wicked soul living behavior is only "wicked soul "ME" easy living" ignorance wicked soul, this is best living, so that there is anything guilty, but proud living, all of other living thing is getting by wicked soul living.

So that wicked soul role is make "revenge and break righteous soul living"

Righteous soul living actor running to the righteous soul living in destination place, all make hard is also wicked soul living actor ignorance is interfere do not running for the righteous soul living.

Actually righteous soul living actor runs to the righteous soul living in destination place hard living is cause of hearing broadcasting from righteous soul living in destination place, then homework, so long righteous soul living actor must do, this is course of living, because righteous soul living in destination place living righteous soul is all being perfect righteous soul living actor, so that in the macro concept world, righteous soul living keep learning being perfect righteous soul living, it is " it shared time with other, help other, but also doing real love other".

So that doing this, all of hard thing is running to the righteous soul living, but to the righteous soul living hard living is wicked soul living actor "revenge and break righteous soul me" so then, if do not strong righteous soul, then righteous soul living actor attacked from wicked soul living actor, so that righteous soul living must be survive from wicked soul is required to live.

To survive from wicked soul, it must do hearing broadcasting, and get creation of knowledge how to free from wicked soul living attacking righteous soul "ME", further more righteous soul living energy increased doing righteous soul living behavior "it shared time with other, help other, but also doing real love other".

Voyage 30days

"Revenge and break energy thinking of wicked soul" around of righteous soul "ME" always locate wicked souls.

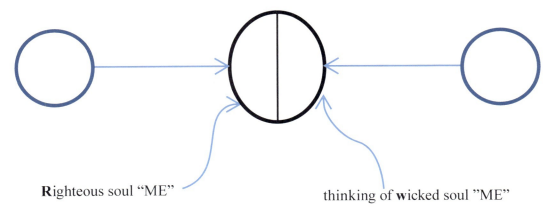

Righteous soul "ME"

thinking of **w**icked soul "ME"

Macro concept world living "ME"

Righteous soul "ME" is master in this novel book, so that righteous soul "Me" feeling is certify what I'm real living.

But truly, if I living with "thinking of wicked soul "ME"" then, my living is with other of wicked soul living actors, because I'm friendly with wicked soul, so that wicked soul living " revenge and break" these energy is produce.

If I see other is same, but as righteous soul "me" point of view is "it shared time with other, help other, but also doing real love other".

But if I living as thinking of wicked soul then, it must be thinking keep repeat to me " revenge and break thinking to the same others just before what I felt anger to others"

Here is very important momentum, in me, governing by righteous soul "ME" then, the anger of wicked soul revenge and break thinking, explain as "forgive and love the thinking of wicked soul"

But if me is living of wicked soul living, then then, the anger of thinking is keep remind me, to do real doing of "revenge and break"

So then if the time is wicked soul governing me, then it must be happened so being of poor living.

In the real living of me, how to live is also, important living.

Just simple living, righteous soul living.

It must be supplied to be energy of righteous soul living, "it shared time with other, help other, and doing real love other"

Create righteous soul living, then righteous soul living "ME" being righteous soul energy is keep increased then, it must be around of "ME" is righteous soul living other, then, in the end, others righteous soul "ME"s are all do same so that real living "ME" is also being "righteous soul "ME" with other, be helped from other, but also, doing real loved from others".

Then righteous soul "ME" feeling "being thinking of wicked soul" then the thinking must be solved as "" forgive this wicked soul thinking then all make clean "me" then sent to the cosmos law courts"

Then I say cosmos law court the result of trials then, please heavenly father forgive me, this is my real living routine.

If not living of governing me is not living of righteous soul, then truly I will be damaged from "thinking of wicked soul revenge and break other" so deep signals, truly strange "thinking of wicked soul" keep going up of before accident remind me, one time was so hard to me but also from other anger, this memory remind me" this is "thinking of wicked soul" so that if real living "me" living in wicked soul then, the man must be follows of all of "thinking of wicked soul" so then, the wicked soul living governing actor, living followed by "thinking of wicked soul".

Righteous soul "ME" and wicked soul "ME" is both, living in me, so that righteous soul "ME" keep watch wicked soul "ME" "revenge and break other". Here other is "righteous soul "ME"" so then wicked soul revenge and break "righteous soul "ME".

What is living?

Righteous soul "ME" is fight between "righteous soul and wicked soul" that is not fight other but just living in me, righteous soul "ME" and wicked soul "ME" survive game, if righteous soul living actor lose then it must be wicked soul occupied in me, then soon, righteous soul "me" is disappeared from "me" then, in the end the real "me" is disappeared from this seen world.

The living of me, is truly living in "me", all is in "ME" not out of me, so then the living of righteous soul living is also living in me.

In this seen world, safe and safe returning to the righteous soul living in destination place, then it must be survive from macro concept world, then in the end safe returning to the righteous soul living in destination place.

truly this truth I felt now know that, so my living also during writing book then it grow to the safe living of righteous soul "ME".

Watch out in me to survive righteous soul so that thinking of wicked soul must watching deep, this is real living.

In the real living, righteous soul "ME" is keep fear wicked soul do "revenge and break me".

Please god righteous soul me, being safe living from thinking of wicked soul, so that this how to live real problem and answer.

Voyage 31days

Today is still hard to me, because of my work place by me; he is living anger to me.

Until now, I understand bad manners to me, is he is now require me to pay back living before world, so I all pray to the god, but now I'm so hard to bear his bad manners.

In this my macro concept world, how to make me hard, so then in this place is 2 years, for 2 years my living has been hard.

Please make him do righteous soul living actor. All his saying is all slander me and others. It was surprised to me, how to this poor man, I'm still he to be righteous soul living actor.

If I follows "thinking of wicked soul" then I'm really ask god to make him out of me.

Heavenly father, please make me move new positon to do work.

Please make change me to new post working.

I tried to make him better living, but not anymore my energy is fail to make him, please god help him to live righteous soul living.

His first name is U, U is living all of talking is cursing others, somehow talking is ignorance useless saying.

I'm so strange with him, but here all of other follow his slander saying accept, my understaffs are liking him, because my post was his, but also my staffs are all northern region place, so that they are all group of norther region, so that I'm full segregated from him.

But I have to manage my team, his behavior keep cut into my team, but also, make me hard to control my team, but also, his behavior to me is " there is no anything to me affect, but try to make hard" his intension make hard to me.

Behavior was peak to me, last year, but still keep make hard me, heavenly father help me from this place, I want to move new position.

Here is U is to me, wicked soul, why U make me hard, U inner world, micro concept world what he has, in him righteous soul living is there, strong righteous soul living is, strangely he living in home, it must be never problems, I don't know.

So then it must be U has righteous soul living also has, because he love family, but also his behavior and tongue is someone be feel good, then maybe I'm wrong doer, my broad mind is shallow and thin. This is all my responsibility to me.

To be all of living overcoming, but also give my real living " it shared time with him, but also help him, and doing real love him" but I'm failing, so then, please save from strong wicked soul, I want to survive from a string wicked soul by me.

Heavenly father please be being living with other righteous soul living, I want to be being living excitement with righteous soul living.

Heavenly father please save from strong wicked soul.

Please save from hell living wicked soul.

I want to live in peace righteous soul living.

Truly I want to write heavy volume but hard to write this book, because wicked soul try to give me, information to write, then the feeling is conflict righteous soul "ME" so that I'm living in righteous soul, so that not any more writing in this book.

I know that living righteous soul is how excitement is, I will keep living in righteous soul living. Please I will not see in the point of wicked soul.

Wicked soul living actor is so fear to me.

Please god keeps saving me eternity.

Heavenly father please make me excitement again.

The name of Jesus Christ amen

Righteous soul living is god lead me to the righteous soul living in destination place.

Wicked soul is to disturb righteous soul living actor runs for the righteous soul living in destination place.

But wicked soul just disturb role only, but wicked soul truly is not care to live on or not, but wicked soul sure to make hard righteous soul living actor hard.

Righteous soul living actor why do living in diligence is this, righteous soul living actor must run over the wicked soul, not to be target to the wicked soul, to do that righteous soul living actor living is the poor & righteous soul, but also its growth to the righteous soul and nothing.

In the end righteous soul & nothing is not seen to the wicked soul, so that righteous soul & nothing is ultimate free from wicked soul.

Righteous soul & nothing can go to the righteous soul living in destination place.

Righteous soul "ME" will reach at the righteous soul living in destination place.

Printed in the United States
By Bookmasters